THE CRISIS OF VISION IN MODERN ECONOMIC THOUGHT

ROBERT HEILBRONER

WILLIAM MILBERG

Published by the Press Syndicate of the University of Cambridge
The Pitt Building, Trumpington Street, Cambridge CB2 1RP
40 West 20th Street, New York, NY 10011-4211, USA
10 Stamford Road, Oakleigh, Melbourne 3166, Australia

First published 1995
Reprinted 1996 (thrice)

Library of Congess Cataloging-in-Publication Data is available.

A catalog record for this book is available from the British Library.

ISBN 0-521-49714-0 hardback
ISBN 0-521-49774-4 paperback

Transferred to digital printing 2002

For Hedy and Shirley

CONTENTS

ACKNOWLEDGMENTS

We are grateful to a small number of friends and colleagues for their contribution to this project, both for their often sharp criticisms of its particulars, and for their support of its overall intent. In particular we would like to thank, in alphabetical order, Ray Canterbery, Peter Gray, Arjo Klamer, Adam Lutzker, Tom Mayer, Donald McCloskey, Tom Palley, Bruce Pietrykowski and Nina Shapiro. We are deeply grateful for their encouragement.

CHAPTER 1

WHAT IS AT STAKE

I

Our intentions in writing this book are two. The first may command disagreement, but not disapproval. It is to place recent developments in macroeconomics into the context of the history of modern economic thought. This seemingly harmless pedagogical exercise, however, conceals a disturbing problem. Let us describe it in terms of the first-year graduate course in the history of economic thought that we have frequently co-taught.

The course covers two semesters, the first of which deals mainly with the dramatic scenarios of the Physiocrats, Smith, Ricardo, Marx, and Mill. This part of the course unfailingly captures the interest of its audience. Who can resist the appeal of these ventures in imaginative logic, in which sociological and political considerations interact with a market-constrained drive for capital to yield the varied trajectories of capitalism that the great economists foresaw?

The second semester begins with the formulations of Jevons, Edgeworth, and Walras. There is, initially, a sense of discontinuity as the narrower concerns of marginalism displace the broader objectives of classical thought, but the audience soon recognizes the underlying continuity of a new "chapter" in the ongoing history of economic thought. The new chapter is more finely analytical in style and less explicitly sociopolitical in content than its predecessor, but it also contains two attributes that legitimate its inclusion within the meta-narrative we call the history of economic thought. The first is an explicit concern for the relevance of its content to the "real" world.

What is surprising is that the new chapter at first seems to lack this attribute. It is true that Jevons writes on the coal question and Edgeworth on the distribution of income required to accommodate the differences in the sensibilities of the various classes and the two genders, but these writings are peripheral to their central, highly abstract concerns with utility; whereas Walras, in our time the commanding figure of the movement, is quite indifferent – even hostile – to the practical application of general equilibrium analysis to political life, despite his own lifelong interest in questions of agrarian socialism.[1]

Yet this seeming exception to our rule that regnant ideas must be relevant to lived economic experience is in fact another vindication of it. Jevons and Edgeworth are key figures in the introduction of marginal analysis to economics, but their statement of it did not actually displace the Millian center of gravity until Marshall's powerful text became its universally recognized exposition toward the end of the nineteenth century. Even more telling, the identification of Walras's name with marginalism would not become commonplace until his highly disengaged approach became a leading force in the postmarginalist, post-Marshallian, post-Keynesian era that will be a central focus of our attention in the chapters to come.

A second, equally important attribute lies in the presence of an identifiable central focus to the economic thought of the period. As we shall see, this focus lies not so much in the analytical framework its authors employ, or in the conclusions they reach, but in the "vision" – the often unarticulated constructs – from which they start. Sometimes, although not necessarily, this vision is incorporated in a seminal synthetic presentation. In the first semester this is accomplished in John Stuart Mill's *Principles of Political Economy*, which projects an eclectic version of classical

1. See, for example, the biographical accounts of Jevons, Edgeworth, and Walras in *The New Palgrave: A Dictionary of Economics* (New York: Macmillan, 1987).

thought that dominates the field from 1848 to 1870; in the second semester, a similar function is performed for the marginalist period by Alfred Marshall's *Economics*, which rules the roost from 1890 until the 1920s.

There follows Keynesian economics, the equivalent of the French Revolution, in the second semester. The focal point again changes, but once more, the two identifying attributes are present: Keynesian economics is quintessentially concerned with the real-world applications of its analytical content, and after a period of confusion, a consensual center emerges, for which Samuelson's *Principles of Economics* may be said to constitute its Millian or Marshallian text. "Keynesian economics" thereupon dominates and gives unity to the economic discourse of its era, as did "marginalism" and "classical political economy" in the eras that preceded it. This is not to claim that other economic schools could not be featured in this overall narrative, Marxian or institutional economics being obvious candidates. It is to make the point that however the chapters of the narrative are identified, they must all manifest the properties of real-world applicability and centrality of focus.

It is this point that sets the stage for the initial problem to which this book is addressed. It is to account for the absence of such a distinct "chapter" in the years that follow the Keynesian era – let us say, roughly, the last quarter century. Thus our bland intention of finding a place for contemporary economics within the larger history of the subject turns out to be much more contentious than might have been anticipated; and leads, indeed, to the second of our larger purposes, whose argumentative character will be immediately self-evident. This is to criticize the direction of economic theorizing in America. The thrust of our criticism is already implicit in the title of our book, and now becomes explicit in the first of the attributes that we have ascribed to economics up to the post-Keynesian period – namely, its continuously visible concern with the connection between theory and "reality." By way of contrast, the mark of modern-day economics is its extraordinary indifference to this problem. At its peaks, the "high theorizing" of the present period attains a degree of unreality that can be matched only by medieval scholasticism. The second purpose of our book must therefore be apparent. It is to serve as a catalyst for change with respect to that attitude.

The Archimedean point to which we shall direct our criticism has already been announced: It is the all-important function of vision for the enterprise of analysis itself. This is a matter to be explored intensively as we go along, but an initial statement seems in order. By analysis we mean the process of deducing consequences from initial conditions, of attending scrupulously to chains of reasoning, and of guarding against the always present temptation to substitute demagoguery for intellectual exchange. By vision we mean the political hopes and fears, social stereotypes, and value judgments – all unarticulated, as we have said – that infuse all social thought, not through their illegal entry into an otherwise pristine realm, but as psychological, perhaps existential, necessities. Together vision and analysis form the basis of everything we believe we know, above all in that restricted but extremely important area of knowledge in which we seek to understand, and where possible to change, the terms and conditions of our collective lives. This is the area to which economic investigation directs its efforts and, accordingly, to which our own critique will be directed.

At the heart of our argument is the contention that "vision" sets the stage and peoples the cast for all social inquiry. One would not have to make such an assertion for the avenues of exploration that we call politics or sociology, for there the elements of vision – our individual moral values, our social angles of perception – are unavoidable starting points for what is to follow. Indeed, vision constitutes the all-important terrain over which intellectual contest is waged in political and sociological controversy. The reason is not that coherence, logic, and other attributes of analysis are unnecessary to support political or sociological inquiry.

It is that politics and sociology – and beneath them, psychology in all its forms – do not possess the lawlike regularities of behavior that demarcate economics as a field of social analysis, investing it uniquely with the characteristics of a social "science." Consequently, chains of reasoning play a relatively minor role in political, sociological, and psychological inquiry compared to that which they play in economics. In no way does this difference make economics prior to, or deeper than, its neighboring approaches, but it does endow it with the capability of developing causal sequences that are often their envy and despair. Analysis has thus become the jewel in the crown of economics. To this we have no objection. The problem is that analysis has gradually become the crown itself, overshadowing the baser material in which the jewel is set. To this we do indeed object, for without the setting there would be no crown.

Our book is not, however, primarily intended to explore the origins or forms of the numerous visionary underpinnings of economics. Its purpose is much more polemical and political. It is to lay bare what we believe to be the disastrous consequences of the failure of the economics profession, especially in the United States, to bear in mind the inescapable presence of vision in defining the tasks that economic inquiry arrogates to itself. These tasks – many in the small, but unitary in the large – entail understanding the central forces within social formations that manifest these regularities. With only trivial exceptions these have been capitalist social formations. Although no doubt the psychic energies that play so large a role within capitalism are discoverable to some extent in all human society, in those other societies the energies will be differently experienced, evaluated, and directed. Thus, what prevents economics from claiming for itself a genuinely universal character is that the vision by which we "see" and "understand" capitalism is not, and cannot be the vision by which we would see and understand tribal, imperial, feudal, or communitarian societies, *if we were ourselves members of those societies*. No analysis of the forms and dynamics of capitalism can hope to be more than superficial if that historical specificity is not made a primary concern.

Yet it is the extraordinary fact that one can only rarely find in the *American Economic Review*, or any of the other prestigious journals of the profession, reference to the specifically capitalist nature of the "system" whose properties are under examination. This omission would be instantly noted were the journals that discussed medieval life never to include the word "feudalism." But in the case of modern economics, the omission of that central identificatory term is taken for granted, never noted, and above all, not seen as itself constituting an important element of the vision that underlies most mainstream inquiry. For it must be clear by now that our concern is not the absence of vision within contemporary economics; no social analysis can be without its "visionary" basis. Our concern, and the change at which our catalytic effort is aimed, is the widespread belief that economic analysis can exist as some kind of socially disembodied study.

This omission has two consequences. The first concerns the extraordinary combination of arrogance and innocence with which mainstream economics has approached the problems of a nation that has experienced twenty years of declining real wages, forty percent of whose children live in "absolute" poverty, and which has endured an unprecedented erosion of health, vacation, and pension benefits.[2] The commitment to full employment legislated in 1946 has been "honored" in these socially destructive years not by vigorous employment-generating programs such as the reconstruction of its cities, but by redefining "full" employment as a higher level of unemployment. New Classical theory, the most recent arrival on the scene, asserts the "optimality" of business cycles. Other, contending theories routinely advise against policy action intended to channel or oppose the spontaneous dynamics of the system.

2. See John Eatwell, ed., *Unemployment in the 1990s* (Armonk, NY: M. E. Sharpe, 1995).

Much of this extraordinary indifference can be traced to the starting point from which modern analysis proceeds. This is the assumption that forces located within "the individual" constitute the conceptual core of economics, a core that is itself immune to further deconstruction, but that can be taken as the foundation on which the sciencelike properties of the discipline rest. As a recent graduate text in microeconomics states, "What most economists would classify as *noneconomic* problems are precisely those problems that are incapable of being analyzed with the *marginalist* paradigm."[3]

Such a statement, along with the microstructure built on it, is more than an analytical device. It is part – operationally, a very important part – of a vision, and moreover a part that performs a conceptual operation Procrustes would have envied. We shall be looking more carefully into the constitutive elements of that larger vision later, but it will convey our meaning if we describe it as a combination of the views of Candide and Dr. Pangloss, a construct of which Marx would have asked, In what never-never-land do such shadow-creatures live?

Our dual objectives of placing recent developments in the context of the history of economic thought and evaluating the state of the discipline as a whole in its present condition are therefore both complementary and interdependent. The history of economic thought is the only "field" in the discipline of economics that allows – or rather, requires – viewing its accomplishments as totalities, not individual parts, and that focuses on the question of the internal divisions as well as the overall trajectory of the social formation as a whole. Our estimation of the dominant vision in contemporary thought is thus diminished by comparison with the visions underlying the large-scale scenarios of the past. What is notable, as we examine this spectrum of visions is the

3. Eugene Silberberg, *The Structure of Economics: A Mathematical Analysis*, 2nd ed. (New York: McGraw Hill, 1990), p. 2.

poverty of reach and depth associated with modern theory. Surely the recognition of the inextricably social roots of all behavior leads to the view that macrofoundations must precede microbehavior, not the other way around, as modern economic thought percieves the issue. Our last, and most contentious point of all, is that we further believe that unless the social setting of economic behavior is openly recognized, economics will be unable to play a useful role as explicator of the human prospect. Once the dismal science, it will become the irrelevant scholasticism. That is what is at stake.

In this book we concentrate on American and British economic thought, to the neglect of Austrian, Scandinavian, French, German (Marxian), Japanese, Italian, and yet other formulations of vision and analysis. This is for two reasons: First, we are writing for a predominantly American and English audience, whose interests, like our own, lie in the resolution of our shared difficulties. In addition, this branch of the History of Economic Thought, although by no means as powerful abroad as it is in the United States and England, nonetheless radiates a worldwide influence. Thus, we believe that the construction of a new "Anglo-American" Classical Situation may have constructive repercussions elsewhere.

CHAPTER 2

CLASSICAL SITUATIONS

I

Our study focuses on the development of modern economic thought, using that phrase to refer to changes in economic theory since the decline of the Keynesian doctrine that exercised a seemingly uncontestable hegemony in the post–World War II era. Since then, we have witnessed a period of internal tension and disagreement for which no parallel can be found in the history of economic thought. The famous Methodenstreit, which erupted in the early 1880s, was effectively over by 1890; in contrast, the unsettled condition of modern economic thought is now more than a quarter of a century old. The once unchallenged centrality of Keynesian thought has given way to a warring camp whose principal, but by no means exclusive, contenders are (in no particular order of importance) Monetarism, rational expectations, Post Keynesian, New Classical, New Institutional, and New Keynesian economics. We shall treat these new schools at varying length in the chapters to come, with side glances elsewhere.

Moreover, this internecine conflict shows no signs of coming to an end. This phenomenon is not only a remarkable occurrence in itself, but also provides the setting for an intellectual puzzle of more than academic interest. The prestige that attaches to economics may far outweigh its achievements, but there is certainly cause for disquiet when the branch of social inquiry most closely associated with political and social policy lacks a firm foundation, in the sense of a core set of beliefs that commands more or less universal assent from both within and outside the profession.

Our hope is to clarify the reasons for this extraordinary disarray. That is not to say that we expect to cut the Gordian knot with a new theoretical approach. Indeed, as the reader knows, it will be part of our argument that the knot is not to be undone by a new advance in method or techniques. On the contrary, we shall attempt to demonstrate that the cause and the resolution of the long-lasting and apparently indissoluble impasse in modern economic thought lies in its pretheoretical vision rather than its postvisionary theory, an approach that summons up the name of Joseph Schumpeter, from whose bold views we take our lead.

Finally, we must confess to a still more ambitious hope. It is not only to offer a plausible rationale for the disintegration of the Keynesian hegemony of the past, but to suggest a general direction in which economic theory must move if it is to rediscover, or recreate, another such period of theoretical unity and developmental thrust. That last ambition is also indicative of the Schumpeterian character of our effort, for it too hinges on the exercise of vision, using Schumpeter's term for the "preanalytic act of cognition" that establishes the style and framework of the analytical structure that vision supports. As to what that vision may be, we must ask our readers to allow us to defer our answer until after we have examined the failures that undermined the former Keynesian center. This task takes us initially not to a further examination of our projected vision, but to the equally important idea of the theoretical center to which all successful visions lead.

II

In his magisterial *History of Economic Analysis*, Joseph Schumpeter invents the term *classical situation* to designate "the achievement of substantial agreement after a long struggle and controversy – the consolidation of the fresh and original work which went before."[1] The concept itself is further elucidated in the text that follows. Asking aloud whether *The Wealth of Nations* ought to be designated as the centerpiece for the first such period, Schumpeter writes:

> Every classical situation summarizes or consolidates work – the really original work – that leads up to it, and cannot be understood by itself. The classical situation of the second half of the eighteenth century was the result of the merger of two types of work that are sufficiently distinct to justify separate consideration. There was a stock of factual knowledge and the conceptual apparatus that had slowly grown, during the centuries, in the studies of philosophers. And, semi-independent of this, there was a stock of facts and concepts that had been accumulated by men of practical affairs in the course of their discussion of current political issues.[2]

To this very general description Schumpeter then appends a footnote: "Like periodization, the setting up of such types is an expository device. Though certainly based upon provable facts, neither must be taken too seriously or else what is intended to be a help for the reader turns into a source of misconceptions. Periods and types are useful only so long as this is remembered."[3] He thereupon utilizes the concept to identify three such periods of summation and consolidation. The first, as we have just seen, is described as belonging to the late eighteenth century, beyond which its content is left unspecified. The second is unequivocally vested in the work of John Stuart Mill; the third "emerged roughly around 1900," and centers around the work of Jevons, Menger, Walras, and later, Marshall.[4]

1. Joseph A. Schumpeter, *History of Economic Analysis* (New York: Oxford University Press, 1954), p. 51, fn. 1. The description comes from Elizabeth Boody Schumpeter, who appends it as a footnote to the text – her husband having never completed the relevant sections of Part I of the *History* in which the concept was to be explicated.
2. Ibid., p. 52. 3. Ibid. 4. Ibid., pp. 380, 953.

Because the idea of a classical situation plays a central organizing function in our book, we must look a little more carefully into what Schumpeter means by the term. Clearly, a "classical situation" represents an important "moment" – perhaps of some duration – in the history of economic thought. It is not, however, that Schumpeter appraised such moments as intrinsically of great worth. On the contrary, it is characteristic of his treatment of them that both their originators and expositors are as often denigrated as celebrated. In the case of his first such moment, that of Smith and Ricardo, its authors are respectively described as "a methodical professor" whose "very limitations made for success," and as the author of "an excellent theory that can never be refuted and lacks nothing save sense." Although the finished exposition of Classical Political Economy is never identified, Schumpeter adds, in passing, that "we still underrate pre-Smithian achievement; we still overrate the 'classics'."[5]

The same largely negative judgment attaches to J. S. Mill, the representative personage of what Schumpeter designates as his second classical situation. Mill is described as one who "underlined" his position "by his attitude of speaking from the vantage point of established truth and by the naive confidence he placed in the durability of established truth." The consequence was a period of "stagnation that was universally felt to be one of maturity of the science, if not one of decay; a state in which 'those who knew' were substantially in agreement; a state in which 'the great work having been done' most people thought that, barring minor points, only elaboration and application remained to be done."[6] To underscore the point, Schumpeter makes a thrust as clearly aimed at the coming ascendancy of the Keynesian doctrine as at the long-vanished supremacy of the Millian: Speaking of the complacency of latter, he writes that "economists, or most of them, were as pleased

5. Ibid., pp. 185, 380. 6. Ibid.

with the results of their handiwork as some of them were to be again in the 1930s."[7]

Thus, classical situations are not in themselves high points of analytical achievement. At best, Schumpeter describes them as moments of "repose" and "finality,"[8] potentially – as in the case of Mill – of a moribund kind. Although Schumpeter carefully avoids evolutionary language in describing the course of economic thought, it would probably not violate his conception if we referred to classical situations as "punctuated equilibria" in the development of that thought – that is, periods when its developmental impetus, evolutionary or not, reached a point of stasis and consolidation marked by widespread agreement as to the kinds of questions to which the doctrine addressed itself and the kinds of answers that it considered most acceptable.

As a consequence of the absence of any analytical content to the idea of classical situations, it is difficult to compare them with other modes of periodizing, or analyzing intellectual progress, such as Popperian "conjectures and refutations," Kuhnian paradigms, and Lakatosian supersessions of degenerative scientific research programs by progressive ones.[9] Unlike these approaches to the clarification of successive intellectual resting points, the idea of classical situations does not lead to a theory of their appearance and disappearance. No attempt is made to put forward the arguments that proved decisive in bringing individual classical situations to stage center, or that forced their subsequent retreats. Indeed, the more we look into the concept that emerges from Schumpeter's study, the more apparent it becomes that this germinal idea – for so we believe it to be – is not an analytical one. Why, then, should we make use of it in a book directed toward the explication of the trend of eco-

7. Ibid. 8. Ibid., p. 754.
9. For an excellent overview see Mark Blaug, *The Methodology of Economics* (Cambridge University Press, 1980).

nomic thought since the 1960s and 1970s – which is to say, toward a period in which analytics has come to be regarded as the very identifying badge of economics itself?

III

There are three reasons. The first is that Schumpeter's is the only attempt to discuss the problem of periodization with respect to economics proper. Popperian, Kuhnian, and Lakatosian methodological perspectives (the last two of which appear considerably later than Schumpeter's work) have often been utilized to give clarity to the sequential development of economic thought, but these efforts inevitably encounter the problem of applying methodological considerations designed to refer to natural science, to the narrative of a social science.

Inevitably this problem begs questions with respect to the resemblance, or lack of resemblance, between natural and social phenomena as research objects. Schumpeter himself was acutely aware of the existence of deep differences between the two, especially with regard to the issue of "ideology" that he regarded as inexpungeably present in social investigation. In our own day we would hold that preanalytical posits are to be found in investigations into the natural as well as the social sciences,[10] but Schumpeter's stress on ideology helps further clarify the crucial term "vision," as he, and also we, use it. Vision is crucial in social inquiry because prominent among the many "precognitive" posits by which we grasp social reality are those that concern the rightness or wrongness, the inevitability or malleability, of the arrangements of power and prestige that we discover in all human societies. These political and moral elements not only color but actually construct such concepts as class, property, and even power itself – concepts that are insepa-

10. See Paul Feyerabend, *Against Method: Outline of an Anarchistic Theory of Knowledge* (London: New Left Books, Humanities Press, 1975).

rable from, and essential for, the analysis of any social order, but for which no analogue of any kind exists in the workings of nature. As must by now be clear, classical situations attain their importance not because they can lay claim to some objective truth, superior accuracy, or usefulness in the constructs they use, but because, for reasons that may be very difficult to defend on "scientific" grounds, they command something like universal assent. Among those reasons we can now place those that concern the social defensibility of the observer's world, a consideration that will not only play its determinative role in construing that world, but in presenting it in a manner that will win consensual agreement. To make the point as strongly as possible, Schumpeter's "moments" in the history of thought attain their importance because they contain the basis for judgmental agreement with respect to the justice and reasonableness of the social order, without which analysis could not proceed.

A second reason for adopting the notion of the classical situation again brings to the fore the immediate purpose of our effort: to describe the breakdown of a particular classical situation that had arisen in Schumpeter's time – the consensus on Keynesian economics. Our task lies not in recounting the narrative of theoretical discontent that has marked these turbulent years, but in seeking to find a rationale for it. There we are guided by another important element of classical situations: the assumption that some central problematic lends a behind-the-scenes unity to the struggle for succession. The very fact that no post-Keynesian point of rest has been found suggests that something is blocking the rise of one or another of the many contenders to a position of general acceptance and hegemony. It is surely an unusual kind of advance when the core of a discipline appears to be less and less, rather than more and more, a matter of general agreement.

But here, too, there is reason to believe that an entry to this obdurate problem may be discovered in the very element that seems to baffle its rational resolution. This returns us once more to Schumpeter's frank admission that in economic matters, only a thin line separates scientific inquiry from ideology – if indeed, the two are ever fully separated. Schumpeter's own words deserve scrutiny:

> Analytic work begins with material provided by our vision of things, and this vision is ideological almost by definition. It embodies the definition of things as we see them, and wherever there is any possible motive for wishing to see them in a given rather than another light, the way in which we see things can hardly be distinguished from the way we wish to see them.[11]

As we have suggested, high among "the definition of things as we see them" are the basic arrangements that establish the social hierarchies and belief-systems of the worlds in which we live. While Schumpeter's concept of ideology may lack precision, its value lies in its emphasis on the sensitive matter of sociopolitical rationalization – an emphasis that sheds light on the dynamics of defending classical situations once they have emerged and find themselves under attack. In what may appear to be an unlikely place, we find some support for this position in Adam Smith. In his essay on the "History of Astronomy," Smith asks, What motive prompts men to pursue the task of theorizing in the first place? His astonishingly contemporary answer is that the purpose of "philosophy" – we would read "scientific methodology" – is "to introduce order into [the] chaos of jarring and discordant appearances, to allay the tumult of the imagination, and to restore it, when it surveys the great revolutions of the universe, to that tone of tranquillity and composure, which is most agreeable to itself, and most suitable to its nature."[12]

Smith is telling us that theorizing reduces our cognitive anxieties before the unknown ("the tumult of the imagination") to

11. Ibid., p. 42.
12. Adam Smith, "History of Astronomy," in *Essays on Philosophical Subjects (and Miscellaneous Pieces)*, ed. W. P. D. Wightman; part of *The Glasgow Edition of the Works and Correspondence of Adam Smith* (Oxford: Clarendon Press), 1980, pp. 45–6.

acceptable levels ("tranquillity and composure"). Classical situations can be regarded as those formulations that reduce the chaos of jarring and discordant social observations, restoring the tranquillity and composure of the political imagination. These situations thus depict moments of psychological rest, whose reigns may be sorely tested by analytical (or empirical) considerations, but whose hegemonic claims are, to an important degree, based on value-imbued considerations.

High among these considerations must be the respective roles assigned to enterprise and to government, especially in a social formation that has always had difficulty in drawing the line between the two. If there is one visionary presumption that sets off Keynes's analysis from all previous classical situations it is his bold ascription to government of a central role in the determination of the momentum of the system itself. This remains a bone that sticks in the craw of the post- (and anti-) Keynesian theorists. There is, to be sure, no lack of analytical reasoning behind this rejection, but it will not surprise the reader that we sense a preanalytical orientation of what Schumpeter would have called an ideological kind: a value judgment with respect to the propriety, as well as the efficiency, of the Keynesian elevation of government's place. We repeat that such an observation does not pass judgment on which side may have the better of the analytical argument, but it helps clarify the inability to reach a new classical situation to replace that which was displaced when Keynesian theory lost its ideological appeal.

There remains a third reason why Schumpeter's concept of a classical situation seems useful – a reason that has to do with the nature of the history of economic thought as a mode of inquiry. In his pathbreaking book, *Stabilizing Dynamics,* Roy Weintraub shows how economic knowledge is socially constructed, and thus how the history of economic ideas must be the tracing out of this construction project.[13] In fact,

13. E. Roy Weintraub, *Stabilizing Dynamics: Constructing Economic Knowledge* (Cambridge University Press, 1991).

Weintraub argues, the "history" of thought is itself a narrative that serves to provide an otherwise missing sense of coherence to the evolution of ideas.

Weintraub takes the example of the stability of general equilibrium models and focuses on the role of the survey article in academic journals in constructing a canonical view on the problem. He analyzes closely a 1963 survey article by Negishi and concludes that

> the history Negishi presented may be different from a history we now might construct; while this seems incontrovertible, it demonstrates that the history of economics *is* constructed. The "success" of a survey may be so great that the field becomes that which was surveyed. Thus we may not be aware, today, of the alternative conceptualizations possible at the time of the survey's constructions, since we see through the survey's lens. The survey truly constructs history.[14]

Weintraub's constructivist approach is equally applicable to the case of macroeconomics in the period since Keynes. Perhaps not surprisingly, historians of economic thought have developed two distinct narratives of how macroeconomics evolved. In the "rational reconstruction," macroeconomics progressed through a succession of analytical advances, each resolving a weakness or flaw in the previously dominant view. Thus Keynesianism was succeeded by Monetarism, which in turn gave way to the rational expectations revolution, which then received further development in the emergence of the New Classical and New Keynesian schools.[15] Central to this telling of the history of ideas is its implicit assumption of progress. Economic ideas move, however slowly, toward truth, and the history of ideas

14. E. Roy Weintraub, "Surveying Dynamics," *Journal of Post Keynesian Economics*, 13 (No. 4; Summer 1991): 526.
15. See, for example, Gregory Mankiw, "Recent Developments in Macroeconomics: A Very Quick Refresher Course," *Journal of Money, Credit and Banking*, 20 (No. 3, August 1988): 436–9; or Stanley Fischer, "Recent Developments in Macroeconomics," *Economic Journal*, 5 (No. 98, June 1988): 294–339.

is the story of the discovery and remedy of the flaws of earlier theories by successive generations of economists.

A second narrative of the history of modern macroeconomics takes a quite different approach. In this view, macroeconomics since Keynes has been a series of misplaced efforts to reestablish neoclassical thought as the dominant approach to issues of income determination, unemployment, inflation, and growth. Accordingly, there are no great differences between Keynesians and Monetarists or their rational expectations descendants. All are linked by their rejection of certain non-neoclassical ideas fundamental to the work of Keynes.[16]

Weintraub would no doubt criticize both narratives, in each case for the implicit or explicit assertion of some objective truth against which all developments can be measured. In his view, the history of economic thought should focus on the construction of ideas, not on their objective or methodological validity, thereby yielding a spectrum of possible histories of thought. Roger Backhouse has rejected this view in favor of a more affirmative approach to the appraisal of economic thought: "Facts may be problematic," he writes, "but to treat everything simply as *fiction* is to abandon what should be one of the main tasks facing the historian of economic thought: to draw conclusions about the merits of different approaches to the study of economic phenomena."[17]

Here the concept of a "classical situation" serves a useful function, by enabling us to ask a question ignored in the par-

16. See, for example, Sidney Weintraub, "Hicksian Keynesianism: Dominance and Decline," in Sidney Weintraub, ed., *Modern Economic Thought* (Philadelphia: University of Pennsylvania Press, 1977); and Malcolm Sawyer, *Macroeconomics in Question: The Keynesian and Monetarist Orthodoxies and the Kaleckian Alternative* (Armonk, NY: M. E. Sharpe, 1982.)
17. Roger Backhouse, "How Should We Approach the History of Economic Thought, Fact, Fiction, or Moral Tale?" *Journal of the History of Economic Thought*, 144 (Spring 1992): 33. See also the exchange between Roy Weintraub and Backhouse in the Fall 1992 issue of the same journal.

alyzing disagreement between an irrefutable but disquieting relativism and a reassuring but vulnerable positivism. The question is why particular forms or formulations of theory achieve their centralizing, stabilizing functions at different times. Once again, in our view, the answer to this question is that the vision underpinning each classical situation serves to reflect or affirm the hopes, or to allay the fears, of the larger community. Thus the adoption of the idea of "classical situations" as the touchstone for theory evaluation enables us to apply some kind of objective analysis to what is otherwise a surrender to the Feyerabendian principle of "anything goes."[18]

Specifically, a focus on vision, within the context of the formation of classical situations, leads almost inevitably to an evaluation of the criteria by which particular theories rise to fill the purpose. In the pages that follow, we show that since the demise of the Keynesian classical situation, American economists have been unsuccessful in moving economics toward such an order-bestowing resolution. This alone is, of course, an evaluation. Ultimately we go a step further, arguing that the failure to attain a new classical situation results from a wrong turn, in terms of vision, that economic thought took when it faced a crossroads in the early 1970s. The nature of that wrong turn, as we see it, must already be apparent, but will be our focus in later chapters.

IV

One last problem remains to be addressed. As we have seen, classical situations are a convenient means of describing consensual moments in the history of economic thought, but they do not in themselves, or in Schumpeter's description of them, enlighten us as to the dynamics of their rise and fall. It stands to reason, however, that these dynamics will be of

18. See Paul Feyerabend, *Against Method,* pp. 27–8.

two kinds. One must be the "internal" problems associated with the analytical exploration of a given depiction of a socioeconomic order. Thus the history of the first classical situation is clearly affected by analytical problems emerging from its general construal of late-eighteenth- and early-nineteenth-century English economic society. Primary among them was the internal consistency of the idea of "value," as the classical canon progressed from Smithian to Ricardian hands – an issue that ultimately played a decisive role in the displacement of Smithian "classical" economics by Ricardian. Other such analytical problems – for example, the long retention of an unsatisfactory formulation for, and the reluctance to surrender the concept of a wage fund – affected the durability of the Millian "classical situation." And it will become apparent that analytical problems of a similar kind played a very important role in explaining the declining authority of the Marshallian mode of analysis and the rise in that of the Keynesian framework.

Thus, internal problems of analytics will occupy an important place in this study, but will not play a vital role in it. Once more, this arises from our deliberate effort to stress the role of vision as the strategic variable in the evolution of economic thought. But it still leaves a question unanswered: To what can we attribute changes in vision? How does one account for the shift from a Smithian to a Ricardian world; or from a Millian to a Marshallian one? There is only one reply that seems adequate to the question. Dissonances must arise between the "view" of the economic world and its immediate workings. The grain fields that climbed the hills in the post-Smithian age; the reform movements of Mill's time; the gradual appearance of a decent standard of working class life by the end of the nineteenth century – all must have exerted their powerful influences in altering the preanalytical cognitive awareness of their generations, and thereby in establishing an impetus to reconstrue the economy. We say "must have" exerted their influence, because there can be no unchallengeable demonstration of so broad an assertion. But unless we wish to eschew all causality to the successive shifts in economic conceptualization, we are left with the need to establish some explanatory scheme, and the changing configurations of perceived "material/political" life experience seems to us the only plausible candidate.[19] Who would deny such a connection between the Great Depression and the rise of Keynesian economics? As Robert Margo has written, "the Depression is largely synonymous with the birth of modern macroeconomics."[20]

Finally, is there some overriding schema, some "meta-history," that marks out the developmental path of economic thought? We see the sequence of Classical Situations as essentially divisible into two segments, the first comprising scenarios of the "classical" variety, exemplified by Ricardo and John Stuart Mill; the second represented by post-classical expositions whose most prominent exemplars are those of Marshall and Keynes. As we will see, the specific exemplifications are not important, insofar as all "classical" and all "post-classical" work displays the identificatory elements of their respective periods.

What constitutes the distinction between them? It is most succinctly described as the contrast between Political Economy and Economics. Political Economy, in turn, is identified by a vision of the social order as comprised of three distinct, but integrally connected, classes – laborers, landlords, and capitalists – with a corresponding analytical focus on the prospects for each. In sharp contrast, our second period is characterized by a vision of the economy as the locus of interaction of disparate actors – individuals or enterprises – whence springs an analytical concentration on forces that determine the incomes of these actors, individu-

19. For a view that places unusual emphasis on the question of *perception*, see Keith Tribe's analysis of the emergence of classical political economy in his *Land, Labour and Economic Discourse* (London: Routledge & Kegan Paul, 1976).

20. Robert Margo, "Employment and Unemployment in the 1930s," *Journal of Economic Perspectives* 7 (No. 2, Spring 1993): 41.

ally or collectively. There is only slight, if any, explicit consideration of this distribution as a class-related matter.

If that description is to have more than superficial plausibility, we must suggest some underlying reason for the change from Political Economy to Economics. We offer two explanations. The first ascribes the change to the displacement of the aristocratic political views, characteristic of the first period, by the increasingly democratic outlook of the second. The aristocratic outlook, in turn, is seen as embodying the view that well-demarcated classes are a natural and necessary condition for any stable social order; whereas its successor democratic outlook tends to downplay, or even to deny the presence of social classes as an inescapable and vitally important property of all social orders. Thus, as we see it, Political Economy and Economics are best understood as interpretations of an evolving capitalist system from the vantage points of two differing historical periods.

Quite independent of this change is a second factor that contributes to the shift in vision. This is the rapid rise in the prestige of natural science – especially that of physics – during the second half of the nineteenth century. Philip Mirowski has shown how the abstract and mathematical character of physical science increasingly became the model for social inquiry for a discipline whose own constitutive "laws" of behavior already tilted it in that direction.[21]

We shall not use this "meta-history" in the chapters that immediately follow, where we attempt to explain the failure of a classical situation to emerge in the half century following the decline of Keynesianism. But the theme of Economics versus Political Economy will reappear later in the book. Here we must be content with our establishment of a crucial point of discontinuity between the two segments of the history of economic thought. Its importance will emerge when we inquire, at the conclusion of our

21. Philip Mirowski, *Against Mechanism* (Totowa, NJ: Roman and Littlefield, 1988), Chapter 1, "Physics and the 'Marginalist Revolution'."

book, into the possibilities for a new Classical Situation in the foreseeable future.

Thus in our study of the evolution of economic visions, we are interested in relating changes in prototypical economic thought – stylistically portrayed as "classical situations" – as conscious or unconscious reflections of a changing socioeconomic, or sociopolitical "reality." Behind this effort, in turn, lies the need to allay the tumult of our imaginations – a need as acute in our times as in those of Smith, as pressing for those who feel the need to conceptualize economic reality as for those who will utilize those conceptualizations as the basis for practical policy. That is the great drama behind this study in economic thought, a drama that we hope will connect politics and economics in ways that render more comprehensible the field's curious record of enlightenment and obfuscation.

CHAPTER 3

THE KEYNESIAN CONSENSUS

I

We turn now to the Keynesian classical situation, not only because this is where our investigation naturally begins, but also because we shall discover within it a clue to the successive unstable equilibria whose unfolding we seek to explain. As with previous classical moments, it focuses our attention on the precursors from whose work the situation emerges – in this case, the marginalist approach that constituted the core concept of economics from the 1870s until the explosive entrance of *The General Theory of Employment, Interest and Money* in 1936.

Immediately we discover a problem that throws light on the difficulties eventually to trouble the successor to marginalism. Marginalism per se is a theory of decision making, in which costs and benefits are weighed precisely, and no certain net benefit is ever forgone. But in practice marginalism has become an amalgam of two approaches to economic theory: approaches that conceal beneath their shared antipathy to Millian economics sharply differing construals of what a "marginalist" vision means. One approach, central to the work of Leon Walras, has stressed the interconnectedness of markets, leading to the vision of general equilibrium as the core concept of economic analysis itself. The other, central to the Marshallian framework, has concerned itself with the process of price formation discoverable in all competitive markets, despite many surface dissimilarities. This process was easily shown to be identical across markets, making the core concept of Marshallian marginalism the "scissors" mechanism of supply and demand.

From these two foci eventually emerged two very different visions of the new classical situation. The Walrasian conception, with its concentration on the systemic unification of markets, retreated from, rather than embraced, a concern with "real life" attributes of specific markets, such as the shapes of supply or demand curves, the operational consequences of time, or problems caused by long-run falling supply curves with their monopolistic implications. Marshallian marginalism, in contrast, focused on precisely such issues, emphasizing the differences in market outcomes brought about by the institutional and historical constraints with which supply and demand had to contend. As a result, although Walras is mentioned in passing in the *Principles* – twice in footnotes, once in an appendix – the concept of general equilibrium does not appear anywhere in the body of Marshall's master text.

In our own day, general equilibrium has come to dominate the marginalist approach to economic analysis, but in the period in which the marginalist vision emerged as the consensual view, it was the Marshallian approach that gained both popular and academic acceptance. At that time, however, no conceptual tensions – certainly none of an ideological kind – marred the general acceptance of marginalism. The classical situation seemed well defined in its rejection of Millian views, with regard to analytical problems such as the source of value and the wage fund, as well as political problems such as its cautious endorsement of a "socialist" direction of capitalist evolution. Both analytically and ideologically, Marshall's tolerant, absorptive approach seemed without, even beyond, challenge. If the absence of interest in general equilibrium was noticed at all, it certainly aroused no concern. Nonetheless, in retrospect, we can see that the victory of marginalism was less complete than it appeared. The idea of an economy whose most important analytical characteristic lay in its condition of overall balance remained as an alternative vision to one of many individual markets without any overarching mechanism of coordination.

Thus the inner tension that was to surface almost immediately in the *General Theory* between its "Marshallian" treatment of such important markets as that for labor or for money capital, and its "Walrasian" treatment of an equality (equilibrium) between aggregate supply and demand in all markets, reflects the failure of marginalism actually to achieve the theoretical unification that seemed to be its most striking feature.

II

We turn next to a description of the classical situation that was to follow the Marshallian view. Here it is well to begin from Marshall himself, to gain a reminder of the nature of the conceptual leap from the *Principles* to the *General Theory*. In Chapter IV of his master text Marshall concerns himself with the meaning of the term Income (we retain in our discussion here his convention of capitalization of important concepts and terms). He speaks of the transformation of its meaning from the "comings-in" of a premonetized family to the revenues (excluding those in kind) of a modern community. He differentiates Income from Capital; he notes the difference between net and gross income; he speaks briefly of certain categories of income (profits, rents, and quasi-rents), and of forms of Capital (circulating, fixed, and others); and thus by degrees proceeds to the conception whose importance is denoted by its designation as subsection 6 of the whole: "Social Income."

"Social income," the subsection begins, "may be estimated by adding together the incomes of the individuals in the society." Marshall then attends to various clarifications of the larger rubric. He distinguishes earned incomes from transfers. He discusses the superior ability of money flows, such as income, to "[give] a measure of a nation's prosperity than that afforded by the money value of its stock of wealth."[1] He brings up the need to allow for depreciation and concludes with typically Marshallian warnings against overly rigid definition.

That done, the concept of Social Income disappears until Book VI, "The Distribution of National Income." Passing mention is made of the concept as a "stream, not a fund";[2] and a footnote on p. 713 begins, "Some years ago the annual income of some 49,000,000 people in the United Kingdom appeared to amount to more than "£2,000,000,000," but moves thereafter to a discussion of its per capita size and its distribution among broad categories of the working class. Beyond these mentions, there is virtually no attention to, or use made of, the concept of social or national income.

Why has Marshall not seized upon this concept whose functional characteristics he obviously recognizes? The answer lies in Chapter II, where he considers the categories of Production, Labour, and Necessaries. The chapter turns first to production: "When [man] is said to produce material things, he really only produces utilities"; thence to consumption, which "may be regarded as negative production."[3] But at this point we meet a decisive statement. Marshall writes:

> Another distinction to which some prominence has been given, but which is vague and perhaps not of much practical importance, is that between *consumer's goods,* . . . such as food, clothes, etc.; . . . and, on the other hand, *producers' goods,* . . . such as ploughs and looms and raw cotton.[4]

Once again an important question is ignored: Marshall rejects, or fails to see, the strategic importance of the distinc-

1. Alfred Marshall, *Principles of Economics*, 8th edition (Philadelphia: Porcupine Press, 1982) p. 80; 8th edition first published in 1920; 1st edition published in 1890 (London: Macmillan Press).
2. Under the index entry *National Income*, of references to "influences affecting growth," there is little of substantive interest.
3. Marshall, *Principles of Economics*, 8th edition, pp. 63–4.
4. Ibid., p. 64.

tion between consumption and investment goods with respect to the behavior of their respective demanders – a distinction that would immediately illuminate and expand the importance of the concept of national income. The reason is not explicitly given in the text because the centrality of the question itself is not recognized. It is not recognized because, as we have already emphasized, Marshallian economics is fundamentally devoted to the exploration of the problem of price, and in this problem the forces of supply and demand play the same roles, and offer the same explanatory entrée with respect to capital or consumption goods.

Thus we can see that the Marshallian vision of economics as an analytical approach to the problem of explaining the formation of individual prices makes irrelevant the question that would emerge as the main object of Keynes's inquiry – namely, how to explain the forces that determine the size of national income. To put the matter differently, from the Marshallian viewpoint the forces that impart momentum and progress to the economy gain their effects as part of the workings of a *social order* in which economic activity is the locus of utility-maximizing exchange that brings moral as well as material betterment.[5] As such, these moral forces continuously and pervasively exert a natural tendency for the upward movement of economic life, save when occasional mismatches or other misadventures temporarily paralyze the "confidence" that is the necessary condition for its normal state of expansion.[6] This is totally at variance with, or perhaps irrelevant to, a conception of income determination along Keynesian lines, in which investment demand has a multiplier effect on consumption and economic output is determined by the level of demand.

Keynesian economics does not emerge from Marshallian, but from post-Marshallian economics. The increasingly poor performance of the economy after World War I brought a growing sense of unease, visible in the redirection of atten-

5. Ibid., pp. 1, 194, 689. 6. Ibid., p. 711.

tion from price determination toward business cycles, a problematic altogether absent from Marshall's text. Economists across Europe and America – Myrdal and Ohlin in Scandinavia, Juglar and Spiethoff in Germany, Mitchell and Hansen in the United States, Tugan-Baranowsky and Kondratieff in the Soviet Union, Robertson and Keynes in England – took the business cycle as the focal point of their studies.[7]

The emergence of business cycle studies as a major object of investigation was not, however, a reorientation of economics sufficiently great to suggest the appearance of a new classical situation. The reason is that the effects of business cycles, however disruptive, were perceived as fundamentally transient and even benign. The ideas that booms might depend on essentially nonrational expectations; that massive unemployment could be both "involuntary" and compatible with an equilibrium of savings and investment; and that a liquidity barrier might prevent the interest rate from clearing the market for money capital were utterly foreign to the view of a system in the protective custody of Marshallian self-correction. To put the same point inversely, the rise in importance of business cycle theory was not in itself enough to pose a fatal challenge to marginalism, insofar as cycles were considered to be more or less regular deviations, rather than long-lasting departures from a norm. Cycles were acknowledged as important, but were attributed solely to exogenous forces and thus placed outside the reach of economic theory. The norm, in turn, was conceived as that volume of economic activity which would be undertaken given marginal revenues and costs – a conception that ruled out the very possibility, save perhaps for brief crises of "confidence," that labor or capital might be deliberately allowed to lie fallow, despite a positive difference of marginal revenues over costs.

7. Joseph A. Schumpeter, *Business Cycles* (New York, McGraw-Hill, 1964), pp. 1123–7. Note that *Business Cycles* (entirely rewritten in the 1930s) was first published in 1913.

III

Our next task, accordingly, is to take the measure of the conceptual challenge posed by the emergence of a theory that put forward all these heretical proposals – namely Keynes's *General Theory of Employment, Interest, and Money.* The content of that theory is too well known to require exposition here. Instead, we shall attempt to examine Keynes's text from the general viewpoint that informs our larger investigation into the formation and supersession of classical situations. In line with our argument, this will involve us more deeply in questions of ideological than analytical differences, always using the term "ideological" in its broad valuation sense. As we shall see, this approach in no way denies the existence or importance of changes in economic analysis, but seeks to reveal their prior grounding in what Schumpeter called "preanalytic" considerations.

Let us begin with what is unmistakably the central break between Marshallian analysis and that of Keynes. It is the displacement of price determination as the essential task of economics by the previously nonexistent task of determining the level of aggregate demand. This is not to say that price determination drops out of the picture in Keynes's analysis, but that it is relegated to a place of secondary importance. To put it differently, the *General Theory* tacitly accepts as a necessary condition for income determination that there exists a satisfactory mechanism for the determination of prices, without which a requisite degree of economic order would not exist; and it acquiesces without demur in the Marshallian analysis of price as the basis of that order-bestowing process.[8]

The central placement of income determination introduces many analytical problems absent from the Marshallian world. The first is how to make determinations of a

8. See Hans E. Jensen, "J. M. Keynes as a Marshallian," *Journal of Economic Issues*, 18 (No. 1, March 1983): 67–94.

previously unrecognized kind, namely the level of "effective demand." This requires changing the focus of analysis from the interaction of marginal utilities and costs which together determine prices in individual markets, to the interaction of flows of national saving and investment that determine the level of national output and employment.

Here is a useful place to separate analytical from conceptual problems, and to advance our contention that it is the latter that set the stage, regardless of how dramatic the activities of the former. Oddly enough, from a conceptual viewpoint there does not seem to be, at first glance, a great difference between utility functions and consumption propensities. Both are based on introspection and casual empiricism: Marshall speaks of the law of diminishing marginal utility as a "familiar and fundamental tendency of human nature," but says nothing further about it of a substantive nature; Keynes describes the propensity to consume as a behavioral pattern "upon which we are entitled to depend with great confidence both a priori from our knowledge of human nature and from the detailed facts of experience," but provides no further support for this assertion.[9]

In fact, however, the conceptual shift entails a consequence of great significance. It is the abandonment of the micro-maximization that provides the fundamental basis for marginalist analysis – indeed, the characteristic that most clearly separates marginalism from the classical situation that preceded it. In its place Keynesian theory postulates a conception of behavior that radically alters both the motivational basis for and the objective outcome of economic activity.

The new view changes the understanding of motivation in two particulars. The first is a shift from an individual-centered to a group-centered conception of behavior. Specifically the conception of economic action as deriving from

9. Marshall, *Principles of Economics*, p. 93; John Maynard Keynes, *The General Theory of Employment, Interest, and Money*, p. 96.

stimulus–response patterns located in all psyches is replaced by a conception of economic action as evidencing social norms for which no lawlike explanation is available. This change carries important consequences: A functional underpinning for economic behavior gives way to a series of ad hoc generalizations for which no such scientific basis necessarily exists. One gets a sense of this when we compare Alfred Marshall's archetypical decision-maker – the boy picking blackberries, balancing his dwindling marginal utility against his rising marginal disutility – with Maynard Keynes's consumer determining his/her savings by reference to the motives of "Precaution, Foresight, Calculation, Improvement, Shortsightedness, Generosity, Miscalculation, Ostentation, and Extravagance," or with the securities trader making his choice for successful investment analogously to picking a photograph that he thinks will be chosen as the prettiest face by a public contest.[10] The "extent" of the market, which is to say, the aggregate demand for commodities, becomes the driving force, not *raretés;* and aggregate demand is less amenable to exact theoretical representation than (idealized) individual demand.

Economic behavior thus becomes less determinate from an analytical view, and economic explanations are accordingly stripped of their "sciencelike" appearance. Curiously, the shift from utility-maximization to propensities actually expands the possibility for empirical investigation, insofar as the tautological character of the former gives way to possibilities for direct measurements of at least some behavioral outcomes – such as marginal consumption/income ratios, or interest rate/investment expenditure relationships. Nonetheless, the analogy between economic behavior and "natural law" – a venerable basis for the differentiation of economics from other forms of social investigation – is made untenable, as considerations of norm-driven mass be-

10. Marshall, *Principles of Economics*, p. 331; Keynes, *The General Theory of Employment, Interest and Money*, pp. 108, 156.

havior are placed at the center of a specifically capitalist social order.[11]

At the same time, the shift from utility maximization to less clearly specifiable motives introduces another element into the view of behavior that is entirely absent from the Marshallian. This is uncertainty. For Marshall, the idea of risk, in both trade and production, is an actuarially determinable chance of adverse outcomes, against which one can find adequate insurance – catastrophes of nature or society perhaps excepted.[12] With Keynes, a margin of uncertainty is an ineradicable aspect of the social process examined by economics, and therefore one that cannot be overlooked in its theoretical clarification. "For Keynes," writes Robert Skidelsky, "most of the things that go wrong – and right – in decentralized market economies stem from the central fact that human beings make decisions in ignorance of the future. Ignorance enters into all the motives for forward-looking action, investing them, at the limit, with the character of dreams and nightmares."[13] The obverse side of this magnification of uncertainty is the elevation of the role of expectations to a hitherto unimagined importance. Again citing Skidelsky: "Economics was, still largely is, built up from the logic of choice under conditions of scarcity. Keynes's vision . . . has to do with the logic of choice, not under scarcity but under uncertainty."[14]

Finally, the admission of an uncertain future not only undoes still further the view of economic inquiry in terms of an orderly calculus, but by that very fact also opens the way for extra-systemic "intervention" as an indispensable element of economic policy. This feature introduces new analytical and conceptual problems of great scope and importance.

11. William Milberg, "Natural Order and Postmodernism in Economic Thought," *Social Research*, 60 (No. 2, Summer 1993): 255–77.
12. Marshall, *Principles of Economics*, pp. 398–400, 613.
13. Robert Skidelsky, *John Maynard Keynes, Volume II: The Economist as Saviour, 1920–1937* (New York: Penguin Press, 1992), p. 539.
14. Ibid.

Market failure had previously been confined largely to matters such as externalities and public goods – problems that have in our day taken on vast importance, but were not generally so regarded in the Marshallian age. After Keynes, market "failure" in the sense of insufficient effective demand, not externalities or price rigidities, was seen as a primary cause for unemployment, the crucial problem of the day. In this way, Keynesian economics laid the basis for the introduction of government as an active generator of economic activity, an expansion of its functions for which no possible justification appeared in the marginalist view. This shift in viewpoint that legitimated the wide enlargement and radical redirection of economic policy, must be understood in the context of the sociopolitical considerations we have just examined, rather than as some spontaneous reorientation of analysis for its own sake.

IV

We next consider the ideological impulse that begins with the shift from utility to propensity analysis, but then moves in a different direction – not toward the nature of economic motivation, but toward the outcome of economic behavior.

Here it is useful to start by noting that formally speaking, there is little difference in the *tasks* posed by Keynesian and Marshallian analytics. As with price determination, income determination depends on the application of behavioral "laws" represented by functional relationships between key variables. Put differently, the determination of effective demand by the interaction of a propensity-driven aggregate demand schedule with an expectations-influenced aggregate supply schedule is not analytically different from the determination of the price of a commodity by the interaction of utility-based supply and demand schedules. Although the Keynesian approach raises a whole range of problems unknown to Marshallian analysis, the skills and techniques of the two exercises are the same: Once having learned the functional relationships in the *General Theory,* an economist adept at Marshallian analysis can readily become a good Keynesian analyst. This would not be the case with a scholar of Aquinian "just" prices or Physiocratic "sterile" occupations who confronted for the first time either Marshallian or Keynesian functional relationships.

We have already noted some of the differences in behavioral understanding that follow from a shift to a propensity-based approach to economic behavior. Here we examine another such consequence of great importance. It is the division of the field of economic inquiry itself into two interpenetrating, but conceptually distinct entities – a division that comes about because Keynes's economics is not easily able to offer a single theoretical framework that embraces both price determination within individual markets and income determination over the nation as a whole. No matter how wide one opens the Marshallian lens, the problem of establishing the volume of aggregate output remains out of focus; and no matter how the focus of Keynes's lens is narrowed, price determination in individual markets never comes into clear view.

This deep divide expresses in a new analytical context the fundamental conceptual distinction between Marshallian and Keynesian economics. We can describe the new context as the difference between "aggregate" and "summative" approaches to the economy as a whole. The summative view, implicit in Marshall and explicit in Walras, derives the national output of the economy by adding up the outputs of its individual markets, each of which is determined by its utility-maximizing drives. There is, therefore, no reason to doubt that the size of the collective output will reflect the same maximization principles that apply to its constitutive elements.

This leads to an approach that does not allow for any difference between such a procedure and the derivation of national output by propensity-driven flows. In particular, the summative view offers no plausibility for, much less explanation of, output levels that can remain in equilibrium although resources of both labor and capital remain involuntarily unemployed. From the Marshallian view, such a combination is a contradiction in terms: The unemployed labor and capital "must" be put to use as long as marginal revenues exceed marginal cost. The difference between the views can be understood in terms of the absence, in the Marshallian framework, of any way of perceiving that markets, in and of themselves, do not reveal such output-determining elements as multiplier interactions, or expectational influences, or "nonrational" liquidity preferences. The difference is not unlike that between a Marxian and a Bohm-Bauwerkian view of capital formation. From the Marxian perspective, capital formation is perceived as taking place in a separate "department" from that in which consumer goods are produced. From the Bohm–Bauwerkian view, capital formation is visible in all kinds of production as an "intermediate" good. From these different angles of vision emerge different analytical problems: overproduction and mismatches from the Marxian "departmental" perspective; roundaboutness and productivity effects from the Austrian "intermediate good" view.

In much the same way, from a Keynesian view we can see that the summative approach does not allow for the possibility that an adding up of individual markets, each considered in its insularity, may overlook interactions that take place in a market system but not in any individual market. Changes in expectations, arising outside the marketplace, or changes in the degree of utilization of resources as a whole, may exert important influences on the configuration of the economy that a summative analysis, Marshallian or Walrasian, cannot discern. The reason is that summative analyses, starting from some "moment" in a timeless existence, have no means of apprehending changes in behavior such as expectational shifts, which are, by their very definition, time-subscripted, or of considering the different configurations that will arise in individual markets and in the dimensions of the system as a whole under different conditions of overall utilization. The upshot is a different view not only of the relation among markets and between an individual market and the overall system, but also of the notion of equilibrium itself. For Keynes, systemwide equilibrium is perfectly compatible with the existence of excess capacity and, more importantly, unemployment. Scarcity, the defining characteristic of the resource allocation process in marginalist thought, is relegated to a minor role in the new framework.[15]

The summative view therefore fails to see all the forces that strategically influence the intersection of supply and demand curves. Here is the entering point of the Keynesian aggregative analysis. Keynesian problems of underemployment equilibria, liquidity traps, multipliers and the like are not "overlooked" in a Marshallian or Walrasian world. They simply do not exist there, because the preanalytic basis for their apprehension has not yet come into being. Market behavior exists as a given, not as a dependent variable.

By way of contrast, the Keynesian view approaches the economy from an angle of entry that emphasizes precisely such effects, with their cumulative or transmarket repercussions. It follows that the aggregative approach, with its emphasis on elements that are unobservable ex ante, renders the process of individual price formation invisible, precisely as the determination of effective demand or the real wage is rendered invisible from a summative perspective. In this way, once again, the preanalytical vantage point establishes the framework within which different problems will come to the fore for analytical investigation. There are, of course, generalizations with respect to "mass" behavior in all economic analysis. Marshall himself makes such a generalization when he says that "the clerk with £100 a year will walk to business in a heavier rain than the clerk with £300 a year."[16] This is not the same thing, however, as postulating

15. See Nina Shapiro, "Keynes and Equilibrium Economics," *Australian Economic Papers* 17 (No. 31, December 1978), pp. 207–23.

16. Marshall, *Principles of Economics*, p. 95.

that individual behavior, such as saving, cannot be depicted solely as the outcome of an individual's utility calculus, but must embrace prior societal determinations that will affect the income, and thereafter, the propensity to consume, of the saver in question.

There remain other instances of analytical distance between Keynesian and Marshallian analysis, such as the role of money in general, and of liquidity preference in particular; the endogeneity of money; the working of the labor market, with its absence of any systematic treatment of the determination of money wages, and yet other problems. These matters have been widely explored in the analytical literature, to which we have nothing to add.[17] As the reader can no doubt anticipate, our own interest lies in the manner in which conceptual a prioris precede these analytical explorations. Monetary considerations, for Keynes, arise from a conception of the world as intrinsically "unpredictable" in a fashion that has no Marshallian or Wicksellian counterpart; and the same can be said, *mutatis mutandis,* for Keynes's view on the labor market or, for that matter, on the role of government itself. We have already noted the contrasting visions that underlay these analytical frameworks, reflecting the historic break that separates Keynes's world from that which preceded it.[18]

V

We therefore turn to a new aspect of our larger subject of the rise of the Keynesian classical situation itself. Our task now becomes that of examining the manner in which the new conceptual framework was made sufficiently palatable –

17. For an overview, see Alan Coddington, *Keynesian Economics: The Search for First Principles* (London: George Allen & Unwin, 1983).
18. For an excellent presentation of Keynes's acute awareness of the historical contingency of his analysis, see James Crotty, "Keynes on the Stages of Development of the Capitalist Economy: The Institutional Foundation of Keynes's Methodology," *Journal of Economic Issues,* 24 (No. 3, September, 1990), 761–80.

perhaps more accurately, digestible – to permit its adoption in place of the framework it sought to displace. To this end, two major emendations were required before Keynes's contribution could serve as a new point of theoretical consensus.

Almost immediately following the publication of the *General Theory* in 1936, incongruous elements began to be removed. One was the threat posed to the long-standing tradition of lawlike economic analysis by the idea of inescapable uncertainty, not as a probabilistic matter that could, to some extent, be neutralized by hedging, but as a series of questions, the answers to which, as Keynes himself wrote, "We simply do not know."[19] The redress of this indigestible element was not achieved by a direct attack on Keynes's perception of risk. The accommodation came about, rather, as the emphasis on uncertainty was gradually allowed to lose the commanding importance it assumed in the *General Theory*. The problem was quietly relegated to the side as a "special case," in a fashion similar to the perverse supply and demand curves in the Marshallian text.

The disavowal was further expedited by the repair of another fundamental difficulty of the Keynesian system. This was the absence of an analytical connection between the older Marshallian universe and the newer Keynesian one. One was soon provided by an analysis that folded the Keynesian model into the prevailing depiction of economics. The amalgamation was presented in J. R. Hicks's famous article on "Mr Keynes and the Classics" which presented Keynesian theory as a two-market equilibrium model, embracing the aggregate flows of investment and saving, and the crucial variables of the rate of interest and the stock of money, but omitting any mention of uncertainty and price level determination, or troublesome problems such as the endogeneity of money and the role of money wages. The

19. Donald Moggridge, ed., *The Collected Works of John Maynard Keynes*, Vol. 14 (London: Macmillan, Cambridge University Press for the Royal Economics Society, 1982), p. 115.

connection was further strengthened by a soon-to-be famous IS/LM diagram which presented the Keynesian model as entirely analogous to the Marshallian.[20]

Here an overlooked aspect of the Kuhnian concept of "paradigm" is helpful. George Argyrous has argued that Kuhn's notion of a paradigm is not merely a general worldview but a view that is exemplified in a precise model: "Without the key element of exemplarship," he writes, "a theoretical approach would be unable to attract members of a scientific community to it."[21] In retrospect, it is easy to identify the example that made possible a unification of Marshallian and Keynesian visions. This was their common representation by a diagram in which two curves intersected – a representation that powerfully suggested a fundamental analogy between the two systems. In the case of Marshall, the diagram represented the price-determining forces of supply and demand. In Keynes, no such convenient and forceful representation at first existed. There was a "supply and demand" diagram, but its purpose was to reveal the inadequacies of the "classical" analysis of investment rather than to establish the *prima facie* validity of his own; and the representation of the new aggregate demand and supply functions used to summarize the principle of effective demand was never given diagrammatic clarity.[22] The Hicksian IS/LM diagram therefore was a stroke of clarificatory brilliance – alas, at the cost of the principle of uncertainty that constituted a new and critically important contribution of Keynes's analysis. We note as a premonition of the unraveling of the Keynesian

20. J. R. Hicks, "Mr Keynes and the 'Classics': A Suggested Interpretation," *Econometrica*, 5 (April 1937): 147–59. The term "classics" in Hicks's title refers to Keynes's (unfortunate) use of that term to describe his opponents in the Marshallian tradition, such as Cambridge professor A. C. Pigou.
21. George Argyrous, "Kuhn's Paradigms and Neoclassical Ecomomics," *Economics and Philosophy*, 8 (1992): 244.
22. The supply and demand diagram is found on p. 180 of the *General Theory*, and the aggregate supply and demand functions are described, not depicted, on p. 25.

consensus that would eventually occur, that Hicks came later to regard his Nobel Prize-winning IS/LM formulation with deep misgivings, and that Keynes himself, who initially approved the Hicksian view, later took issue with its treatment of uncertainty and money demand.[23]

A further rapprochement between the marginalist and Keynesian views was accomplished in 1948 with the appearance of Paul Samuelson's textbook *Economics*.[24] The text was immediately popular, and remains the prevailing pedagogical representation of "Keynesianism," including the presentation of its analytical core in the form of another simple Marshallian diagram, in which a 45-degree line of income/cost is intersected by an aggregate expenditure curve to determine the equilibrium level of national income. Of perhaps greater importance, the text overcame the gulf between Marshallian and Keynesian views by consigning the first to a "micro," and the second to a "macro" section. Neither section discussed the problems of the other, and the two approaches were presumably reconciled by being bundled into a single textbook.

This separate but equal treatment of a macro system and a micro system opened the way for a legitimation of governmental policy, especially with respect to fiscal measures, that was totally new and largely antipathetic to the pre-Keynesian

23. In a letter to Hicks, Keynes at first did not reject the Hicksian model. See Moggridge, ed., *The Collected Works of John Maynard Keynes*, Vol. 14, pp. 79–81. For a discussion of Keynes's later expression of dissatisfaction with the Hicksian rendering, see Skidelsky, *John Maynard Keynes, Volume II: The Economist as Saviour, 1920–1937*, pp. 539, 614–16; and Donald Moggridge, *Maynard Keynes*, 1st edition (Toronto: University of Toronto Press, 1976), appendix. Hicks's own misgivings are found in John R. Hicks, "Some Questions of Time in Economics," in Anthony Tang et al., eds., *Evolution, Welfare and Time in Economics: Essays in Honor of Nicholas Georgescou-Roegen* (Lexington, MA: Lexington Books, 1976), pp. 140–1. Also see John R. Hicks, "IS-LM: An Explanation," *Journal of Post Keynesian Economics* 3 (No. 2, Winter 1980–1), pp. 139–54.
24. Paul A. Samuelson, *Economics*, 1st edition (New York: McGraw-Hill, 1948). The book is now in its 12th edition.

classical situation. From the perspective of vision, this policy orientation was surely as substantial an impact of "Keynesianism" as the evolution of a macroeconomics on a par with micro; and indeed, was the preanalytical basis on which that analytical departure was based. In turn, as we have mentioned earlier, the underlying stimulus for such a legitimating vision was undoubtedly the trauma of the Great Depression, which dominated politics in all capitalist countries.[25]

Last, but certainly not least, the original Keynesian doctrine was also modified in another, more constructive way. Early on, it was recognized that one of its difficulties was the handling of dynamics. In its original exposition, the Keynesian depiction of successive equilibria was essentially treated as a Marshallian exercise in comparative statics, because the definition of saving and investment as identities precluded a clear representation of the path of income change. Keynes's explanation that investment and saving were brought into equilibrium via changes in the level of income conflicted with the definition of saving and investment being equal at all levels of income. Nor did the introduction of the idea of ex ante inequality and ex post equality, taken from Knut Wicksell, do much to clarify matters, insofar as there was no operational specification of the time periods denoted by "ex ante."[26]

The problem was ultimately overcome by Roy Harrod, who introduced as the central problematic issue the determination of equilibrium rates of growth of output instead of levels of output – a change that did not seriously affect the analytics of the IS/LM diagram, but that profoundly altered the vision of the process that "Keynesian" economics repre-

25. Note that in the 1930s many non-Keynesian economists advocated an expansionary fiscal policy. But this was not closely tied to an explicitly altered economic vision. See J. Ronnie Davis, *New Economics and the Old Economists* (Ames: Iowa State University Press, 1971).
26. See Robert Heilbroner, "Saving and Investment: Dynamic Aspects," *American Economic Review*, 32 (December, 1942): 827–8.

sented.[27] The *General Theory* was not concerned with long-run processes, except in a historical, evolutionary perspective. Over a less historic span the prevailing approach to dynamics was largely that of business cycle analysis, in which variations of output were represented as self-correcting departures from a norm that rose only secularly and was largely beyond policy control. In sharp contrast, the Harrodian analysis placed rates of change in output at the center of analysis, with the result that changes in the saving rate, technology, education, and "human capital" became target variables for policy. Although Harrod's work did not gain prominence until after Keynes's death in 1946, in many ways it constitutes a completion of Keynes's vision. Growth itself, formerly perceived as a process determined by exogenous events over which no kind of deliberate control could be exercised, was now placed within the reach of macroeconomic policy founded on Keynesian ideas.

VI

Thus, by the early post-World War years a true classical situation had appeared. Keynes's "general" theory had become accepted by economists in a way that must have more than fulfilled its author's hopes, although at the expense of a considerable weakening of its originality and power. Much as the Millian model had earlier been modified to rid itself of the wage fund, the faint remainders of a labor theory of value, and a vague endorsement of a postcapitalist social order; or as the worlds of Jevons, Menger, and Walras were broadened to include Marshallian quasi-rents and other in-

27. Roy F. Harrod, "An Essay in Dynamic Theory," *Economic Journal*, 49 (March, 1939): 24–33. Also see Roy F. Harrod, *Towards a Dynamic Economics* (London: Macmillan, 1948), Lecture 3. At about the same time, U.S. economist Evsey Domar formulated a similar model. See Evsey D. Domar, "Capital Expansion, Rate of Growth and Employment," *Econometrica*, 14 (April 1946): 137–47.

stitutional considerations, so the disruptive, uncertainty-centered model of the *General Theory* was converted into a pastiche of ideas, not so much blended as permitted to coexist, with their mutual contradictions and inconsistencies allowed to go unresolved. The result was termed "bastard keynesianism" by Joan Robinson, a term still used by those economists who lament the deviations from Keynes's theory among Keynesians.[28] The watering down of Keynes was later described in less cutting, but more explicit fashion by Harold Somers in a book review in the *American Economic Review:*

> The name of Keynes is anathema in some circles. . . . One publisher even boasts that his elementary textbook contains no mention of Keynes. . . . All is not lost. There is available a very competent economist called Macro. This economist, Macro, is most versatile. He . . . encompasses everything that Keynes taught, might have taught, and would have denied teaching.[29]

Out of these conflicts and contradictions would emerge the problems that eventually brought to an end the Keynesian classical situation. That would not be the case, however, for a time. By the early 1970s, following a quarter century of largely unchallenged Keynesian hegemony in the English-speaking world, the prevailing view was that economic theory was now complete and needed only econometric substantiation.[30] In retrospect one is reminded of John Stuart Mill's famous declaration in 1848: "Happily, there is nothing in the laws of Value which remains for the present or any future writer to clear up."[30] Mill's classical sit-

28. Joan Robinson, *Economic Heresies* (New York: Basic Books, 1971), p. 90. To further confuse matters, the group that uses this term calls itself "Post Keynesian"!
29. Review of Somers, *Macroeconomics, Measurement and Analysis, American Economic Review*, 54 (No. 2, Part I; March 1964): 138.
30. J. S. Mill, *Principles of Political Economy* (Toronto: University of Toronto Press, 1965), p. 456. First edition published by Parker and Co., 1848.

uation, however, still had a long way to go, whereas the demise of Keynesianism had already begun. "By about 1980," writes Alan Blinder, a staunch defender of Keynesian theory, "it was hard to find an American academic macroeconomist under the age of 40 who professed to be a Keynesian. This was an astonishing intellectual turnabout in less than a decade."[31]

As a final comment on the impending unraveling of the classical situation of the postwar era, it should be noted that Keynesianism was never accorded the same status abroad, with the possible exception of England. The Scandinavian nations had already accepted the views of Myrdal and Ohlin, in many ways more radical than those of Keynes; the French embraced an ad hoc economics compounded of a monetarism and a *dirigisme* espoused by de Gaulle; Germany pursued a mixture of welfare policies and conservative financial rules; the Dutch and Belgians were of necessity primarily concerned with international economics where Keynesian thought had a relatively small role to play; and Italy was engaged in a multisided effort to encourage the industrial development of its north, and to break the economic backwardness of the *mezzogiorno.* Thus the Keynesian classical situation was very much an Anglo-American phenomenon, as were also the Marshallian, Millian, and "Classical" situations before it. This reminds us that the familiar "history of economic thought" of this book is not the only such: There are German, Austrian, French, Italian, and yet other sequences of economic theory, not to mention the overarching influence of Marx, perhaps the single most influential economic "history" of all.

We conclude our chapter with this somewhat humbling reminder for two reasons: first, to avoid falling into the trap of thinking that Anglo-American history is of the same importance to all nations as it is to ourselves; and second, to

31. Alan S. Blinder, "The Fall and Rise of Keynesian Economics," *The Economic Record* (December, 1988): 278.

assert that despite the considerable number of such histories, we can find in all of them powerful visions establishing "resting places" of their various analytical sequences. That is an assertion beyond demonstration in this short volume, but perhaps the mention of Marx's work will suffice to make plausible our contention that "powerful" economic theory is always erected on powerful sociopolitical visions; and that theory retains its power over our intellects only as long as its underlying visions continue to mobilize our moral sympathies.

CHAPTER 4

THE GREAT UNRAVELING

I

How shall we explain the decline of Keynesianism? An obvious way is to pursue the analytical tensions and inadequacies with which we have become generally familiar in our last chapter. These difficulties will have an important role to play in our subsequent discussion. But they constitute an aspect of the problem that has already been explored by many writers, to which we have nothing of significance to contribute.[1] In examining the decline of the Keynesian consensus, we propose, therefore, to follow our theme of the interplay of vision and analysis. Analytical problematics interest us, in this study, insofar as they reflect the manner in which we construe the economic problem itself. The advent of the Keynesian classical situation clearly arose from a radical change in that construal in the face of the Great Depression. What remains to be demonstrated is that the subsequent dissolution of the Keynesian consensus also reflected changes in the existing socioeconomic conditions, and the alteration in economic vision that arose from that state of affairs.

We must therefore begin our inquiry by considering, in shorthand fashion, the historical background against which the decline of the Keynesian classical situation must be viewed. The economic consequences of the end of World War II hostilities were anticipated with considerable trepidation by the Allies. In the United States, expectations for

1. See, for example, John R. Hicks, *The Crisis of Keynesian Economics* (New York: Basic Books, 1975).

postwar unemployment were alarming. In Great Britain, the crushing defeat of Churchill in the elections of 1945 announced a new Labour regime whose program was aimed primarily at preventing the economic dysfunctions of the prewar period. Out of similar pessimistic economic expectations, France likewise voted in a left-wing government. It is not too much to say that capitalism itself appeared to be on trial, and that one of the motives for the Marshall Plan was to forestall the advent of a "socialist" Europe.

All the more important (because it was completely unexpected) was the buoyancy that began to appear in Europe as soon as the immediate postwar devastation came under control. By the end of the 1950s, Germany, whose immediate postwar industrial production was only one-third of its 1938 level, had become the "economic miracle" of Europe. Ten years later, it would rise to the unquestioned first rank of economic power. Against all expectations, the "cockpit" of Western Europe established an Iron and Steel Community in 1951, a European Economic Community in 1957, and a European Common Market in 1967. Only the United Kingdom lagged behind in this triumphant reassertion of capitalist vigor, and there were special reasons, having to do with its wrenching loss of imperial power, that accounted, at least to some degree, for this exception.

Thus, by the late 1950s, the specter of a collapse of European capitalism gave way to a growing conviction that a rejuvenated Europe was likely to become the most powerful economic entity in the world. The efforts of the United States to encourage European integration in order to avert any possibility of Germany's veering off to join the Soviet camp have been described as *too* successful: By the mid-1960s "fortress Europe" began to compete with imports coming from the United States, and by the 1970s European firms were competing globally with U.S. multinationals.[2] Meanwhile, an

2. Fred Block, *Origins of International Economic Disorder* (Berkeley: University of California Press, 1977), Chapters 5 and 6.

even more astonishing resurgence was visible in the East. After a few years of acute economic suffering, the Japanese economy began to evince a remarkable economic vitality. By the 1950s, the rate of growth of Japanese GDP per worker was over 5.5 percent, and by the 1970s had risen to just under 10 percent, the highest in the world.[3] Earlier, Taiwan had evinced a similar vitality, and by the early 1960s the first signs of a successful transplantation of capitalism to the Asian mainland were already visible in South Korea and Singapore.

In this global surge of capitalism, the American economy displayed laggard tendencies, in both its overall rate of growth and in its pace of technical advance, the latter given shocking immediacy by the successful Russian space shot in 1957. Nonetheless, the first two postwar decades were unquestionably a time of widespread economic contentment in the United States. Real family income rose by 52 percent between 1959 and 1969, real per capita consumption by 31 percent.[4] These were years of high living compared to the past and extravagant prospects for the future. Even the achievements of the Soviet Union served the prevailing economic optimism by providing an example to be surpassed, as well as a rationale for military expenditures that served, in some measure, as a substitute for European and Japanese private and public investment.

Thus if we can plausibly ascribe the rise of Keynesian economics to a perceived challenge to the capitalist order, the postwar decades provided at least as dramatic a reason to alter the framework within which Keynes's theory would be judged. It may well be, as we shall later see, that Keynesian policy provided a foundation on which European and Asian welfare economics was at least partially based, but during the years in which capitalist governments recovered their sense

3. Jeffrey Williamson, "Productivity and American Leadership: A Review Article," *Journal of Economic Literature*, 29 (No. 1, March, 1991), table 1 (p. 57).

4. *Economic Report of the President* (Washington, D.C.: U.S. Government Printing Office), February 1994, p. 301.

of confidence, explicitly Keynesian policies, such as deficit spending, played only a modest role in the resumption of capitalist growth.[5] Indeed, looking backward, perhaps the most evident reminder that Keynesian economics was still the prevailing "classical situation" was that governments everywhere recognized the existence of a "macrosystem" to be dealt with separately from the "microsystem." But this recognition was of far less importance than a growing European commitment to a new active engagement of government in the microstructure, ranging from Germany's *sozialmarktwirtschaft,* to French encouragement of industrial "rationalization" and French–German–British participation in industrial ventures such as the Airbus. At the same time, the new versions of capitalism in Japan, Taiwan, Singapore, and South Korea were from the beginning openly *dirigiste* in policy, and even less dependent on Keynesian fiscal measures.[6]

Thumbnail histories cannot serve as arguments in explaining changes in the visions behind economic theory or policy. The preceding sketch is intended to do no more than remind us of the extent and depth of the contrast between the pre- and postwar setting within which economic thought was situated, a contrast easily forgotten in the near half-century that has passed. The degree of influence that can be attributed to a change in background conditions is always a matter of uncertainty, but when the change is large, any inquiry must surely begin by taking cognizance of its presence.

II

We turn now to considering the fate of the Keynesian classical situation from the perspective of its analytical content. It

5. Gerald Epstein and Juliet Schor, "Macropolicy in the Rise and Fall of the Golden Age," in Stephen Marglin and Juliet Schor, eds. *The Golden Age of Capitalism: Reinterpreting the Postwar Experience* (Oxford: Oxford University Press, 1991).
6. Alice Amsden, *Asia's Next Giant: South Korea and Late Industrialization* (New York: Oxford University Press, 1989).

will not come as a surprise that the principal finding of the successive evaluations of Keynesianism from this viewpoint have been negative. The conclusion that emerges with great force is that the Keynesian approach is deeply, perhaps even fatally, impaired by an analytical framework that is inadequate to its task, mistaken in some of its main causal sequences, and misleading with regard to the overall dynamics of the economic system as a whole.

The inability of Keynesian doctrine to present a coherent theory of inflation was the first, although not the most decisive of these analytical critiques. The Keynesian model in its original form contained no systematic treatment of inflation on a par with that of unemployment, and in its eclectic IS/LM variant, equilibrium in the goods and money markets did not include the determination of the price level. This gap was filled in 1958 by the well-known work of A. W. Phillips, who discovered that the rate of unemployment in the British economy between 1861 and 1957 was inversely related to the rate of change in the wage rate.[7] For a considerable time the ensuing Phillips curve was generally felt to have provided not only the missing foundation for a theoretical treatment of inflation but also a seemingly solid basis on which economic policy could be based.

This apparent remedy for a serious shortcoming of Keynesianism was always regarded with suspicion, insofar as it was rooted in the particular historical evidence of England, rather than in the logic of the IS/LM formulation. As James Tobin put it, the curve was "an empirical finding in search of a theory, much like a Pirandello character in search of an author."[8] The Phillips curve was, however, given its more serious test in independent theoretical challenges mounted by

7. A. W. Phillips, "The Relation Between Unemployment and the Rate of Change of Money Wage Rates in the United Kingdom, 1861–1957," *Economica*, No. 2, 1958.
8. James Tobin, "Inflation and Unemployment," *American Economic Review*, 62 (No. 1, Parts 1–2; March 1972). Paul Samuelson and Robert Solow did find some confirming evidence in the U.S. data. See Paul Samuelson and Robert Solow, "Analytical Aspects of Anti-inflation Policy," *American Economic Review*, 50 (No. 2, May 1960): 177–94.

Milton Friedman and Edmund Phelps, and was questioned on empirical grounds by Robert Gordon and Robert Lucas.[9] The critics argued that the level of unemployment would not reflect the nominal but the real wage, and would therefore tend, after a period of "money illusion," toward an unchanging unemployment–inflation relationship. Friedman maintained that the Phillips curve would always extend vertically from the "natural" rate of unemployment, a term later changed to "nonaccelerating inflation rate of unemployment" (NAIRU) to avoid an implicit designation of the relationship as unchangeable or socially optimal.

To what extent was the Phillips curve controversy decisive in bringing about the fall of Keynesianism? The answer depends considerably on whether we consider the matter from the perspective of analysis or vision. From an analytical viewpoint, wide agreement exists that NAIRU relationships, shifting with changing conditions in the labor market, with inflationary expectations, and with adjustment for supply shocks, are superior to the previous idea of "fixed" Phillips curves.[10] For example, Robert Lucas wrote in 1981 that "Keynesian orthodoxy is in deep trouble, the deepest kind of trouble in which an applied body of theory can find itself: It appears to be giving wrong answers to the most basic questions of macroeconomic policy."[11] Even the well-known Keynesian, Axel Leijonhufvud, admitted:

9. Milton Friedman, "The Role of Monetary Policy," *American Economic Review*, No. 1, 1968; Edmund S. Phelps, "Phillips Curves, Expectations of Inflation and Optimal Employment over Time," *Economica*, No. 3, 1967; Robert Gordon, "Wage–Price Controls and the Shifting Phillips Curve," *Brookings Papers on Economic Activity*, 2 (1972); Robert Lucas, "Econometric Policy Evaluation: A Critique," in Karl Brunner and Allan Meltzer, *The Phillips Curve and Labor Markets* (Amsterdam: North-Holland, 1976).
10. See Robert Topel, "What Have We Learned from Empirical Studies of Unemployment and Turnover?" *American Economic Review*, 83 (No. 2, May 1993): 114–15 , and Robert Gordon, "Comments," in Jerome Stein (ed.), *Monetarism* (Amsterdam: North-Holland, 1976), p. 54.
11. Robert Lucas, "Tobin and Monetarism: A Review Article," *Journal of Economic Literature*, 19 (No. 2 June 1981): 559.

> When the American inflation picked up steam, the misbehavior of the Phillips-curve and the inflation premium in nominal interest rates became obvious for all to see. Monetarists, who had predicted these things by reasoning from the neoclassical anticipated inflation model, made enormous headway within the economics profession and without. Keynesians, who had continued to argue the usefulness of the Phillips-curve and to pooh-pooh the empirical relevance of the anticipated inflation model, lost face and lost influence. It was a debacle. A bad enough debacle so that the profession proclaimed the long controversy a Monetarist victory and, by and large, turned its interest elsewhere.[12]

For reasons that we shall quickly come to, however, from the vantage point of vision what appears as a weakness becomes a strength. Thus Alan Blinder wrote in 1987 that "the Phillips curve, once modified to allow for supply shocks, . . . has been one of the best-behaved empirical regularities in macroeconomics,"[13] to which he added in the following year: "The charge that empirical Keynesian models were, in Lucas and Sargent's words 'wildly incorrect' is, well, wildly incorrect."[14]

What we have here is an instance of the determinative importance of preanalytical considerations in accepting or rejecting an analytical proposition. On the face of it, we have two contrasting judgments on whether or not the econometric evidence denies the plausibility of the Keynesian model. But prior to this analytical disagreement is the fact that the two protagonists openly espouse opposing views with regard to Keynes's economics in general – Lucas rejecting, and Blinder accepting its basic coherence and relevancy. This places both analytical judgments under suspicion of being

12. Axel Leijonhufvud, "What Would Keynes Have Thought of Rational Expectations?" UCLA working paper, Series A, No. 177, July 1983, p. 5.
13. Alan S. Blinder, "Keynes, Lucas, and Scientific Progress, " *AEA Papers and Proceedings*, 77 (No. 2, May 1987): 133.
14. Alan S. Blinder, "The Fall and Rise of Keynesian Economics," *The Economic Record* (December 1988): 282.

influenced by the visionary positions of their proponents, whether methodological or "ideological." While this situation is not unique to economics or even social science generally, it is particularly acute in the economics field since the era of Keynesian consensus. From Lucas's view, the admitted inability of the original IS/LM model or of the underlying Keynesian functions to yield NAIRU-like results is sufficient evidence to pronounce a guilty verdict with respect to the validity of the theory whence these defects spring. From Blinder's view, the adaptability of Keynes's concepts to institutional relationships that did not exist, or had not yet come into importance, at the time the *General Theory* was being written – for example, the wide use of inflation-transmitting wage indexing through cost-of-living adjustments – suggests that the theoretical underpinnings of Keynesian economics are validated precisely because they can be adapted to a wider range of behavior-shaping influences than Keynes himself intended.

The disagreement is not just about the relevance of Keynes's framework, but about the role of the economist qua social scientist. For Lucas, the distinctive attribute of economics lies in its "scientific" foundation in rational individual choice. Accordingly, the obligation of the economist is to pursue the logic of this foundation. For Blinder, realism and historical adaptability of the framework are more important than strict adherence to ontological principle. One unexpected outcome of these conflicting views is the differing importance accorded to research itself, insofar as it is used to justify policy. For Blinder, who supports a Keynesian interventionist approach, the economist's responsibility is to pursue precisely such research. Lucas, who holds a contrary view, asserts that "the politics and the political role that economists play has had a very bad effect on macroeconomics."[15]

15. Quoted in Arjo Klamer, *Conversations with Economists* (Savage, MD: Rowman and Littlefield Publishers, 1983), p. 52.

In this conflict of opinions there does not seem to be any objective basis for determining which verdict is the appropriate one. Success or failure lie in the eye of the beholder, rather than in objective criteria. Economists take recourse to arguments other than those based strictly on logic and empirical evidence. Considerations of vision appear of crucial significance – not in resolving the problems to which economic theory addresses its attention, but in determining what are to be the criteria by which the theory itself is appraised.

III

We can deal much more rapidly with the second frequently cited reason for the unraveling of the Keynesian classical situation: its failure to include a concept of stagflation – the simultaneous experience of recession and rising inflation – in its spectrum of macroeconomic outcomes. The problem can be dealt with succinctly because it is essentially a variant, or perhaps a special case, of the Phillips-curve inadequacy.

Stagflation is a condition that would have been considered a contradiction in terms by most economists prior to its advent in the 1970s.[16] During those years, inflation appeared to lose its formerly clear-cut relationship to the level of employment. In the United States, for example, as the rate of unemployment rose from 4.8 to 8.3 percent between 1970 and 1975, the rate of inflation rose steadily from 5.4 to 9.6 percent.[17]

There is no question that Keynes had not anticipated such a state of affairs, being always much more focused on the problem of deflation than inflation. This is not to say that he ignored inflation entirely, just that he did not see it

16. The exception that proves the rule is Jacob Viner's review of *The General Theory*. See Viner "Mr. Keynes and the Causes of Unemployment," *Quarterly Journal of Economics*, 51 (1936–1937): 147–67.
17. *Economic Report of the President* (Washington, D.C.: U.S. Government Printing Office, 1993).

as a problem in the context of the Great Depression.[18] As before, therefore, Keynesian macrotheory in its original form can be judged a failure insofar as the theory neither predicted, nor easily accommodated, these new economic conditions. The Council of Economic Advisers would report in 1974, "There is no simple explanation for this price behavior which was the most extraordinary in almost a generation and which confounded the Council and most other economists alike."[19]

Also as before, however, Keynesian theory can be judged a success insofar as it can be altered to include stagflation within the general framework of its central propositions, the alterations taking the form of allowance for increased bargaining power of labor. In turn, these changes can be traced back to a marked strengthening of the ability of labor to withstand the pressure of unemployment – a change brought about in the United States by the dramatic increase in unemployment insurance coverage between 1960 and 1980 from 43.7 to 87.2 millions, and by informal "labor accords" between unions and management in the major manufacturing corporations beginning in the period immediately following World War II.[20] In Europe a much more far-reaching strengthening of labor's bargaining position resulted from the general emplacement of codeterminative and other policies aimed at enhancing the security of national trade unions. The result was to set the stage for an unprecedented enhancement of trade union bargaining power in Europe and, to a lesser extent, in the United States.

18. In a 1940 essay Keynes in fact expressed strong concerns about the inflation that might ensue after the removal of price controls. See John Maynard Keynes, *How to Pay for the War: A Radical Plan for the Chancellor of the Exchequer* (New York: Harcourt, Brace, 1940).
19. *Economic Report of the President* (Washington, D.C.: U.S. Government Printing Office, 1974).
20. For unemployment insurance, see *Statistical Abstract*, 1987, table 559; On the role of labor accords see Michelle Naples, "The Unraveling of the Union-Capital Truce and the U.S. Industrial Productivity Crisis," *Review of Radical Political Economics*, 18 (Nos. 1–2, 1986): 110–31.

Thus, some part of the advent of stagflation should be attributed to institutional developments that were neither intended by nor directly traceable to Keynesian policies. As with the case of the Phillips curve, it seems unreasonable to blame Keynesian doctrine for a failure to foresee this change, and therefore to anticipate its consequences. According to Epstein and Schor, the "golden age" of postwar growth among advanced capitalist countries was "both produced by and conducive to a permissive policy stance. By contrast, periods of slow growth and fragility result in pressures for policy restraint, which in turn reinforce an economy's poor performance."[21]

It follows from the foregoing that one can interpret stagflation as involving causal linkages for which Keynesian policies may be a necessary but certainly not a sufficient antecedent. The analytical connection in this case is therefore at best an ex post, not an ex ante relationship. On the other hand, the phenomenon of stagflation itself can be seen as reflecting a changing socioeconomic framework in which Keynesian economics appears as a powerful political force, both in the formulation and in the reception of national economic policies of many sorts. In this case, as with the Phillips curve, Keynesian economics bears an indirect responsibility for real-world economic effects that are difficult to understand from a non-Keynesian perspective. This does not deny, however, the existence or importance of such effects.

Quixotically, then, stagflation has contributed to the fall in the prestige of Keynesian economics, rather than to a recognition that the phenomenon of stagflation is most easily explicable in the context of a regime of "successful" macroeconomic policy. From this vantage point, the success or failure of Keynesian economics again hinges on whether the

21. Gerald Epstein and Juliet Schor, "Macropolicy in the Rise and Fall of the Golden Age," in Stephen Marglin and Juliet Schor, eds. *The Golden Age of Capitalism: Reinterpreting the Postwar Experience* (Oxford: Oxford University Press, 1991), pp. 149–50.

criterion is that of analysis or vision. Analytically, Keynesianism is at best adaptable to stagflation, certainly not anticipatory of it. From the standpoint of vision, however, Keynesianism takes on a powerful explanatory significance, for it enables us to understand the socioeconomic requirements in which stagflation – a contradiction in pre-Keynesian terms – could come to dominate the scene.

Stagflation has come to an end with the political and economic events of recent years. The bargaining strength of labor in the advanced industrial countries has been threatened in part by the rise of international competition. Hence, it is likely that economics will become increasingly concerned with international rather than national economic issues, and that whatever classical situation becomes dominant in the foreseeable future will be correspondingly more transnational in form. We mention this prospect now if only to make the point that any successful economic theory will have to be judged in terms of both its internal consistency and its external conceptualizing power, precisely as in the rise of Keynesianism.

Of these two judgments, analysis will surely be that which most attracts the investigatory skills of the economics profession. But vision will continue to play its all-important prior function of establishing the boundaries, depth, and social significance of the problematic view itself. This is a task for which no criteria of logic exist – rather, only conceptions of greater or less clarity, and interpretations of more or less persuasiveness, all rendered ambiguous insofar as their persuasiveness and clarity will vary according to the predilections of each observer. Of such frail stuff is made the iron determinations by which the world is run.

IV

We turn next to a consideration of the Keynesian treatment of money, another frequently cited reason for the decline in its generally received prestige. Once again, there is substance to the charge from an analytical perspective, but the more important reason for the criticism seems to involve the conceptual implications of the Keynesian view of money and monetary policy.

As with the Phillips curve and the problem of stagflation, the attack on the Keynesian treatment of money hinges on the cause of inflation. Indeed, the original impetus to the reassertion of monetarism was its apparently better predictive performance during the 1970s. In Milton Friedman's words, "Inflation is always and everywhere a monetary problem in the sense that it is and can be produced only by a more rapid increase in the quantity of money than in output."[22] Thus a restrictive fiscal policy alone is insufficient to curb inflation. More recently, the attack has abandoned the importance of predictability, as the assumption of a stability of the demand for money and velocity – the key precept missing from Keynesian theory – has proved in recent times to be much less evident than formerly thought. As a case in point, monetarists did not predict the fall in inflation after 1982, nor the severity of the recession in that year.[23]

This concession, however, does not dispose of the monetarist dissatisfaction with Keynesian theory. The root of the problem seems to lie, rather, in different conceptions of the larger economic order itself. In the Keynesian system, inflation is ultimately a monetary symptom of a nonmonetary condition – namely, overutilization of existing productive capacity. In monetarist theory, in sharp contrast, inflation is always a problem of an oversupply of money compared with the existing "real" state of affairs. Thus, all major inflations are at root monetary. The issue, therefore, is not whether money is an integral element of the original Keynesian view: One would hardly expect the author of *A Treatise on Money* to have propounded a book of diagnosis and remedy in

22. Milton Friedman, *Money and Economic Development* (New York: Praeger, 1973), p. 28.
23. Thomas Mayer, *Monetarism and Macroeconomic Policy* (Aldershot, NY: Edward Elgar, 1990), pp. 70–7.

which monetary aggregates and policy were matters of no consequence. It is, rather, how to fuse a coherent view of the function of money with the static approach to equilibrium that emerged as part of the Hicksian IS/LM version of the Keynesian classical situation.

Two aspects of the IS/LM presentation led to serious difficulties. The first was the static nature of the IS/LM approach in general, which ruled out the inescapably dynamic properties of a monetary analysis. Hicks himself recognized the difficulty when he wrote in 1976, with respect to the IS/LM model, "I must say that the diagram is now much less popular with me than I think it is with many other people. It reduces *The General Theory* to equilibrium economics; it is not really *in* time."[24] Monetary analysis, however, as Hicks realized, requires time. The reason, as Paul Davidson puts it, is that, by virtue of its function as a store of value, "money [is] a one-way (present to future) time machine."[25] Thus, any analytical presentation of the effects of money must follow what Meir Kohn calls "sequence analysis" in its treatment of causal variables.[26]

Against this widely accepted call for a time-laden analysis, what we find as a central feature in the IS/LM version of the *General Theory* is a timeless equilibrium approach in which attention is focused on the intersection of "motionless" money supply and demand curves rather than on their continuously changing configuration, placement, and even interdependence. In all fairness, it must be said that this static representation itself derives from Keynes's decision to present the savings–investment relationship as an identity,

24. John R. Hicks, "Some Questions of Time in Economics," in Anthony Tang et al., eds. *Evolution, Welfare and Time in Economics: Essays in Honor of Nicholas Georgescou-Roegen* (Lexington, MA: Lexington Books, 1976), pp. 140–1.
25. Paul Davidson, *International Money and the Real World*, 2nd edition (New York: St. Martin's Press, 1992), p. 65.
26. Meir Kohn, "Monetary Analysis, the Equilibrium Method, and Keynes's 'General Theory'," *Journal of Political Economy* 94 (No. 6, 1986): 1193.

with the antidynamic consequence of treating the multiplier relation as "logical" – that is, timeless. Kohn is correct in writing that "the internal contradictions of the *General Theory* . . . led to a nightmare of confusion among professional economists from which we are only now beginning to emerge."[27]

Once again, however, the analytical problems posed by Keynes's method do not pose insuperable obstacles or condemn his general approach to irrelevance. Keynes is explicit in declaring that his new approach was "chiefly concerned with the behaviour of the economic system as a whole . . . [where] the actual level of output and employment depends not on the capacity to produce or on the pre-existing level of income, but on the current decisions to produce which depend in turn on current decisions to invest and present expectations of current and prospective consumption."[28] Insofar as the *General Theory* is mainly concerned with the chronic problem of underemployment characteristic of his times, Keynes's analysis clearly refers to a situation in which the causal effects of monetary changes are, by virtue of the situation, minimized.

But there is no analytical contradiction in specifying that the upward sloping portion of the LM curve becomes increasingly inelastic – and therefore influential – as we move to higher levels of output. Such an analysis is comparable to the case of similarly shaped supply curves for resources, in fixed or sticky supply, where the price effect of a given shift in demand varies depending on the level of demand. Thus, according to some monetarists, the Keynesians simply overstated the interest elasticity of money demand and understated the interest elasticity of expenditures; in other words, the IS/LM framework gives "monetarist" results if the shapes of the two curves are correctly drawn. To admit that

27. Ibid., p. 1192.
28. Donald Moggridge, ed., *The Collected Works of John Maynard Keynes* (London: Macmillan, Cambridge University Press for the Royal Economics Society, 1982), pp. 22–3.

much is to deny that there is an analytical error in the Keynesian formulation, and to propose tacitly that there may well be an error in one's "vision" of behavioral response to monetary stimulus.[29]

A deeper incompatibility rests with the Keynesian postulate that a persisting ("equilibrium") condition of underemployment can exist in the first place. This follows from a number of preceding assumptions, of which the most important with respect to the monetary mechanism is the existence of the very liquidity threshold that sets a lower bound to interest rates. This reduces the efficacy of monetary policy as an incentive, although not as a deterrent: It was often said in rationalizing Keynesian monetary policy that one could not push with a string, but could certainly pull with one.

Liquidity preference thus creates a zone of monetary impotence, vitiating the relevance of monetary policy over the range of high unemployment situations at which it is most clearly aimed. It is precisely here that the Keynesian vision strikes a crippling blow at the Marshallian assumption of an economy always capable of being raised to a level of full utilization. The blow comes through the admission that if an economy does not spontaneously reach that level, it cannot count on recourse to the one measure of government intervention that is always granted legitimacy – namely, loosening the constraint of an inadequate supply of money.

Thus, the "problem" posed by the Keynesian approach to money did not lie in its analytical inadequacies, which were real enough but not irremediable. It lay in its preanalytical view of the economy as a social mechanism subject to a chronic dysfunction for which a more powerful medicine than monetary policy was likely to be required. That the interest rate was not a real variable bringing investment and saving into balance is a view that clashed directly with the position of the pre-Keynesian "classicals" against whom

29. See Karl Brunner and Alan Meltzer, "An Aggregative Theory for a Closed Economy," in Jerome Stein, ed., *Monetarism* (Amsterdam: North Holland, 1976), p. 57.

Keynes contended, and with that of the post-Keynesian "New Classicals" to whom we shall turn in our next chapter.

The success of the monetarist "counterrevolution" was thus partly due to its association of Keynesianism with the idea that "money did not matter." The fault here does not lie entirely with the monetarists, but also with the Keynesians' interpretation of Keynes.[30] As Harry Johnson wrote:

> [Keynes's] followers – which means the profession at large – elaborated his history-bound analysis into a timeless and spaceless set of universal principles, sacrificing in the process much of his subtlety, and so established Keynesianism as an orthodoxy ripe for counter-attack.[31]

Keynesian economics, it cannot be said too often, begins from a premise that was anathema to the pre-Keynesian vision of capitalism – namely, that capitalism, by virtue of its twentieth-century institutional characteristics, was chronically vulnerable to persisting conditions of inadequate expenditure flows. It is that vision which decisively separates the Keynesian classical situation from the Marshallian vision, and it is this same irreconcilable difference that leads to the differing importance accorded to monetary manipulation in both. In Keynesian analysis, as in Friedman's, money matters, but it matters in different ways and to different degrees because the properties of the social order in which it exerts its effects are differently conceived.

V

There remains a last, and in our view, most important analytical difficulty in the Keynesian classical situation. This is its bifurcation of economic analysis into two coequal but not contiguous modes of inquiry, one continuing the Marshal-

30. See, for example, Alvin Hansen's influential book, *A Guide to Keynes* (New York: McGraw-Hill, 1953).
31. Harry G. Johnson, "The Keynesian Revolution and the Monetarist Counter-Revolution," *American Economic Review* 78 (May 1968): 1–14.

lian approach to the economy as an intricately interconnected congeries of markets, comprehensible as one gigantic total market; the other adding the concept of a system whose dynamics could not be portrayed as originating in a single market or group of markets. Probably because Marshall was aware of pitfalls in the simple aggregation of individual market outcomes, his attention was almost exclusively focused on questions of partial, rather than general equilibrium.

In the present context of examining the causes for the Keynesian decline, this emphasis acquires a new and decisive significance. At issue is the priority to be accorded to each kind of equilibrium. In the Marshallian analysis, all economic questions are described and analyzed in terms of the behavior of individuals, whose interaction constitutes the only cause of the outcome in the individual markets that depict the processes under examination. In Keynesian analysis, as we know, collective determinations often take precedence over individual behavior by strongly influencing it. We owe the sharp distinction between individual and collective analysis to Paul Samuelson's famous *Foundations of Economic Analysis,* published in 1947, which framed the issue in terms of the "micro" and "macro" that have become permanent additions to the economic vocabulary.

This posed both a clarification and an obfuscation of analysis itself. The clarification lay in the convenience, especially with respect to policy, of conceptualizing the economy as "containing" two distinct kinds of equilibration mechanisms. The obfuscatory part lay in the absence of the lawlike scientific underpinnings of utility maximization – the source of the presumably "scientific" character of microeconomics – in the larger processes of macrodetermination. In recent times, this scientificity has come under increasingly critical scrutiny. Against this must be ranged the more immediately apparent failure of Keynesianism, whether in its original or in its more eclectic versions, to find a fully developed, rational-maximizing substratum beneath its crucial behavioral functions. The "animal spirits" that dominate the

Keynesian investment function, the depiction of uncertainty in terms that defy probabilistic analysis, the "propensities" that dominate consumption behavior – all lack a behavioral basis that accords with the logic of choice that pervades the Marshallian view. If economics is to be based on, and bounded by behavior that displays the attributes of such a logic, Keynesian macroeconomics is thereby excluded from being considered on a parity with microeconomics. The result, in Alan Blinder's words, is that Keynesian economics finds itself "an infidel in the neoclassical temple."[32]

In contrast to our previous discussions, there appears to be no means of overcoming or bypassing this analytical problem. Keynesian behavioral premises do not derive from, and cannot be reduced to those of pre-Keynesian analysis. The recognition of this impassable analytical barrier, however, rests on an essential supposition: namely, that the scientificity of economics lies in the properties of its microfoundational base. This is a matter we shall examine with particular care in our next chapter, when we examine the arguments of several new directions of contemporary theory that have sought to establish themselves on such a base. Suffice it to state in advance that the premise has come under attack from many angles, the most important of which is the long-recognized tautological property of its key definitional terms "rational," "maximizing," and "utility."

Here we risk the assertion, a little in advance of its full demonstration, that the fall of Keynesian theory from its position of unquestioned hegemony cannot in fact be explained by its absence of a clear-cut microeconomic basis, although it is often attributed to that fact alone. We hope that by now we have made a convincing case for our argument that the decline of Keynesian economics, although no doubt aided by its analytical shortcomings, is grounded in visionary or ideological considerations. As to what these may have

32. Alan Blinder, "The Fall and Rise of Keynesian Economics," *The Economic Record* (1988): 285.

been, we end this chapter where we began it – by recalling the extraordinary contrast in the social and political backgrounds out of which sprang the economic analyses of the 1930s and early 1940s, and those of the 1950s and 1960s. In the chapter to come, we examine the various forms taken in a search for a model that would more fully reflect the spirit and the problems of the later period, leading down to the present day. As we have said, all historically based explanations are inherently contentious. Nonetheless, it seems to us that the larger issue to which our study is addressed cannot be elucidated without taking into account the influence of the historical setting in shaping the perceptions and preconceptions that its "classical situations" would bring to the fore.

CHAPTER 5

THE INWARD TURN

I

Virtually unchallenged as the consensual center of macroeconomics during the first two decades of the postwar period, Keynesianism became by the late 1960s a model in general disrepute. In his brilliant overview of what happened, Gregory Mankiw begins with an intriguing aspect of the Keynesian downfall: The disregard – even the "derision" – to which Keynesian doctrine was increasingly subjected was almost entirely confined to theoretically oriented academic circles.[1] In policy-oriented centers, public or private, its essential validity and usefulness were largely unquestioned. The reason is that the emerging criticisms were impossible to translate into operational models capable of illuminating economic problems or performing more successfully than the Keynesian macroeconomic prototypes they sought to displace.

Mankiw makes clear, however, that this disparity raises as many questions as it answers. Five centuries ago, he points out, a navigator who steered by the Ptolemaic system would have guided his ship more successfully than one who followed the still poorly understood Copernican one. This raises the possibility that the poor operational performance cited by the remaining Keynesian practitioners only reflected a Copernican revolution in its early stages – a warning against the easy conclusion that because the anti-

1. Gregory Mankiw, "A Quick Refresher Course in Macroeconomics," *Journal of Economic Literature* (December 1990): 1658.

Keynesian models were not of practical use, they must have been based on erroneous theoretical underpinnings.

At the conclusion of his survey, however, Mankiw advances another possibility: "Copernicus had a vision not only of what was wrong with the prevailing paradigm, but also of what a new paradigm would look like. In the past decade, macroeconomists have taken only the first step in this process; there remains much disagreement on how to take the second step."[2]

The comparison serves very well to set the stage for our task in this and the next chapter. We must begin, as in our earlier consideration of Keynesian thought itself, with a brief overview of the analytical issues at hand. Once again, however, that is only a preamble to our main task which is to inquire into the preanalytical conceptual basis – the vision – whence the analytical criticisms arise. Moreover, in our present task the inquiry cannot stop here. The searching question posed by Mankiw requires that we carry our investigation further, looking for an explanation of why the assault against Keynesian doctrine failed to produce a paradigm powerful enough to replace it.

II

In our initial survey of the Keynesian classical situation, we identified four principal criticisms. Three of them were connected with the difficulties of accommodating inflation-related concerns within a framework in which "real" rather than monetary influences were given clear priority. Indeed, in the typical Keynesian representation in the 1950s and 1960s, the only decisive role accorded to money-driven behavior was the creation of a zone of monetary impotence, once interest rates fell below the level established by whatever liquidity requirements happened to prevail.

As we have also seen, many of these shortcomings could be remedied by the introduction of expectations-augmented

2. Ibid.

Phillips curves and a "natural" rate of unemployment within the general configuration of an IS/LM presentation. That is, no irreconcilable distance separated the Keynesian framework of a "macro system" from the special concerns of the monetarist school. Robert Gordon has characterized this as "the paradox of convergence without agreement"[3] – that is, the possibility of summarizing both sides of the debate in terms of the slopes of the two curves. This is confirmed by the views of both Friedman and Tobin that the monetarist–Keynesian differences were largely of an empirical, not a conceptual, nature.[4]

We need not pursue the monetarist criticism further. Rather, the near-compatibility of monetarism and Keynesianism raises an issue closer to our central interest: Why did monetarism not become the natural successor to Keynesianism? Why did it not play the organizing theoretical and policy-oriented role that Keynesian economics had occupied until the late 1960s?

There are a number of answers to the question. The first is that the empirical relationship between the money supply – especially M1 – and the levels of general prices, income, and unemployment became increasingly unreliable in the 1970s. A breakdown in the empirical relation among money, prices, and income that had begun in the 1970s reached a climax in 1981–1982. Money demand was wildly overestimated, radically disconfirming the monetarist transmission mechanism and resulting in the "Volcker crisis" of 1982. This disconfirmation alone might have fatally undermined the possibility of using a monetarist model as the central reference point for theory and practice.[5] But there were

3. Robert Gordon, "Comments," in Jerome Stein, ed., *Monetarism* (Amsterdam: North-Holland, 1976), p. 53.
4. James Tobin, "Friedman's Theoretical Framework," in Robert Gordon, ed., *Milton Friedman's Monetary Framework: A Debate With His Critics* (Chicago: University of Chicago Press, 1974). See also Friedman's "Comments on the Critics," in the same volume.
5. Thomas Mayer, *Monetarism and Macroeconomic Policy* (Aldershot: Edward Elgar, 1990), pp. 70–3.

additional reasons as well. One lay in a growing change in Friedman's accommodating statements with respect to the mutual compatibility of Keynesian and monetarist views. As Tobin pointed out in 1965, Friedman's earlier premise that "money mattered" was increasingly expressed, perhaps loudest by his detractors, as "only money mattered." The difficulty was compounded by Friedman's espousal, in his 1968 presidential address to the American Economic Association, of an unvarying, announced target rate of the growth of the money supply as the central – indeed, only – macropolicy required to achieve stabilization, regardless of the state of the economy.[6] This stance had strong underpinnings in the vision of an economy that operated optimally "on its own," save for the unavoidable role of government in providing a monetary base. Keynesian opposition was likewise rooted in its vision of an economy that required government intervention to ensure growth and stability.

A third problem was the lack of rational-choice microfoundations of monetarist theory. As economic science became increasingly identified with the rational-choice approach in the 1970s and 1980s, Monetarism fell out of favor, especially among younger economists. From the outset, Monetarists had been concerned with capturing broad empirical regularities, a methodology made famous in Milton Friedman's landmark "Essay on Positive Economics," and exemplified in his *Monetary History of the United States*."[7] The irony is that the initial willingness of the monetarists

6. James Tobin "The Monetary Interpretation of History," *American Economic Review*, 55(1965): 464–85; Milton Friedman, "The Role of Monetary Policy," *American Economic Review*, 58 (No. 1, March 1968): 1–17. Friedman had proposed a monetary rule well before 1968, but his presidential address received broad attention.
7. Milton Friedman, *Essays in Positive Economics* (Chicago: University of Chicago Press, 1953); Milton Friedman and Anna Schwartz, *A Monetary History of the United States, 1867–1960* (Princeton: Princeton University Press, 1963). This approach perhaps reflected Friedman's old-Chicago school neoclassicism, too informal even for many Keynesians. Palley has argued that theoretical and empirical monetarism

to do battle with the Keynesians on their IS/LM terrain, hurt the Monetarist cause when they later rejected that framework.

Other analytical problems may have further weakened monetarism's claims to a hegemonic position. But in our view a fourth issue was decisive. Analytical difficulties do not pose insurmountable problems for classical situations, as a moment's reflection reveals with respect to the inconsistencies and deficiencies in Smith and Mill, not to mention Marshall and Keynes. What seems ultimately of crucial importance is the capacity of a consensual model to embody the sociopolitical values and the historical prospects of the period in question. Here we find a striking difference between the Keynesian situation and that of monetarism. As we have mentioned more than once, Keynesian doctrine depicted an economic condition of ever latent, and often manifest instability, for which no remedy existed except strong public intervention. This corresponded very closely to the ethos of the years in which Keynesian doctrine took shape and became the guiding principle for economic policy. By the same token, however, the failure of monetarism to generate a new classical situation should not blind us to its successes. The intuitive appeal of the quantity theory of money quickly resulted in a broad popularity of monetarism among policy makers. Most macroeconomic theory since the 1970s has had a distinctly monetarist bent, including even the "New Keynesian" theory of the 1980s and 1990s.

Indeed, as the public focus shifted from a concern with employment and income to worries over inflation, Keynesianism faltered, offering only "fiscalism in reverse" – that is, fiscal restraint – which proved to be of no value in combatting the inflationary surge. As a result, both its theoretical and its policy-related prestige diminished. With this

should be considered distinct. See Thomas Palley, "The Monetarist Counter-revolution: A Reappraisal," *Eastern Economic Journal* (Summer, 1993).

failure, the monetarist belief in long-run monetary "rules" struck an increasingly popular chord. The business world jumped on what seemed the prognostic value of Monetarism; suddenly the money supply figures were all that mattered. Later, politicians latched on, and a simple monetarism was espoused and practiced by leaders of a number of countries, including the United States, the United Kingdom, Germany, Israel, and Chile, among others. As Michael Bleaney has put it:

> Money supply control seemed to promise a new era of financial stringency in the public sector and an altogether more discriminating attitude towards its activities. Whereas the experience of the depression and war, together with the intellectual backwash of the Keynesian revolution, had long sustained a pronounced growth of public expenditure and intervention and the development of an extensive welfare state, by the end of the 1960s the rising burden of taxation was beginning to eat a hole in people's pockets and a reaction set in against the cost and dubious justifiability of various state expenditures. For the political right, Monetarism was to become the way to link popular dissatisfaction about taxation, public generosity and the suspicion that it was being abused by 'scroungers' with the other source of great anxiety, inflation. Thus despite the technical and involved nature of the academic debate, in the wider world Monetarism became a key component of a right-wing critique of the Keynesian/social–democratic consensus of the postwar period, a consensus which had been characterised by great optimism about how the state could be used to improve the lives of the community.[8]

All this has a quixotic ending. One would think that the congruence of monetarist doctrine with the emerging conservative sociopolitical view would have acted to seat it firmly on the vacant throne of prevailing economic theory. And so it well might, had it not been for one thing. The throne of economic thinking was usurped by another con-

8. Michael Bleaney, *The Rise and Fall of Keynesian Economics*, p. 141.

tender, analytically less vulnerable and ideologically even more congenial to the conservative temper of the times. This was the axiom of rational expectations, which Mankiw describes as "perhaps the largest single change in macroeconomics in the past two decades."[9]

III

Unlike the expectations in Friedman's monetarist model, which were "adaptive," or formed by extrapolating past expectations into the future, rational expectations were wholly based on currently formed estimates of the future. As the idea achieved wider acceptance among economists, rational expectations became increasingly recognized not as a school of thought, but as a technique that applied optimization analysis to the issue of expectations formation.

Insofar as market behavior depends on currently formed expectations, the axiom has an unavoidably tautological property in that the market's movements could not have occurred had marketers' expectations-guided actions not been what they were.[10] This tautological element has been recognized by many critics, including Cagan, Colander and Guthrie, and Tobin, who have made it a central basis for their attacks on the hypothesis.[11] The criticism, although valid, may be beside the point. In discussing the impact of the rational expectations hypothesis, Mankiw goes on to say that the hypothesis considered by itself has no more – and no less – empirical content than utility maximization.[12] Al-

9. Mankiw, "A Quick Refresher Course in Macroeconomics," p. 1648.
10. James R. Wible, "The Rational Expectations Tautologies," *Journal of Post Keynesian Economics*, 5 (No. 2, Winter 1982–3): 200.
11. See Phillip Cagan, "Reflections on Rational Expectations," *Journal of Money, Credit and Banking*, 12 (Part 2, 1980): 827; David Colander and R. Guthrie, "Great Expectations: What the Dickens Do 'Rational Expectations' Mean?" *Journal of Post Keynesian Economics*, 2 (No. 2, Winter 1980–1): 228; and James Tobin, "How Dead is Keynes?" *Economic Inquiry*, 15 (No. 4, October 1977): 466.
12. Mankiw, "A Quick Refresher Course in Macroeconomics," pp. 1648, 1649.

though Mankiw does not use the term, his characterization makes the axiom a heuristic whose usefulness is not to be judged by the economic modeling possibilities it opens up, but by the construals of reality it makes possible.

It is, therefore, wrong to denigrate the axiom because it is based on the notion that the agents of the economy possess as farsighted and accurate estimates of economic dynamics as do the wisest economists, a statement usually followed by acerbic remarks as to the reliability of the "wisest" economists' foresight. Such reactions are beside the point in the same way that ridicule of the clearly tautological character of utility maximization misses the purpose for which the axiom exists.[13] That purpose is to enable us to perceive an otherwise invisible logic in economic events – a logic that allows us to imagine the outcome of economic dynamics ex ante, or at least to reconstruct them ex post, on the basis of systematic reasoning. The point can perhaps be most clearly made by asking how much understanding one could bring to the operation of a market system if one possessed no concept of "utility maximization." In the same way, rational expectations must be accorded that initial understanding if it is to be fairly appraised as an attack on the Keynesian paradigm.

We begin in this fashion, not because we wish to offer a blanket defense of rational expectations, any more than that of utility maximization. On the contrary, our purpose is to set the stage for examining more carefully the nature of all heuristics, which is to say, of all construals of the "chaos" of raw reality – William James's famous "buzzing, blooming confusion" of uncategorized nature. That purpose is to make us aware not only of the indispensable purposes served by "constructing" social reality, but to alert us as well to the unintended consequences that inevitably accompany its original order-bestowing usefulness. These side effects may take

13. The theory of revealed preference in fact rendered utility per se noncentral to the analysis of consumer choice; see H. S. Houthaker, "Revealed Preference and the Utility Function," *Economica,* 17 (May 1950): 159–74.

many forms, some perhaps subliminally intended by those who project structured meanings into the world – including, we hasten to add, ourselves; and others unnoticed or unmentioned. The "world," natural as well as social, thereby assumes meanings as well as shapes, not as an illicit aspect of the social construction of reality, but as a matter of necessity, even of right, in order to make the world morally as well as psychologically habitable.[14]

These matters begin to play a strategic role at this stage of our narrative. One such vision-related problem was made immediately apparent as the consequence of the rational expectations hypothesis. It was the conclusion, inextricably implied by the tautological character of the hypothesis, that policy was incapable of altering the course of spontaneous market behavior. Rational expectations takes as its central posit that market participants act in the market on the basis of the full range of their information. This market situation always remains unknowable in its full complexity, but marketers, obedient to their "rational" natures, construct what they foresee as the most likely shape of things to come. This does not entail that each and every agent must thereby predict market outcomes accurately and may not therefore suffer losses, but it does entail that actors' expectations, taken in their totality, will accurately predict market outcomes because these expectations will, by their translation into action, determine how the market in fact behaves.[15]

Two conclusions follow, both trivially and yet of major consequence. The first is that no "representative" individual can "beat" the market, save by good luck, a conclusion widely applied to stock market analysis.[16] The second, far more conse-

14. See Robert Heilbroner, "Was Schumpeter Right After All?" *Journal of Economic Perspectives*, 7 (No. 3, Summer 1993): 92–5.
15. See Steven Sheffrin, *Rational Expectations* (Cambridge University Press, 1983), p. 9; and Sheila Dow, *Macroeconomic Thought: A Methodological Approach* (Oxford: Basil Blackwell, 1985), pp. 149–51.
16. See, for example, Sanford Grossman, "On the Efficiency of Competitive Stock Markets Where Traders Have Diverse Information," *Journal of Finance*, 31 (1976): 573–85.

quential implication is that no *nonmarket* observer can beat the market, insofar as there is no reason to believe that such an actor would be significantly more foresighted with respect to market outcomes than any representative agent. If we now make this nonmarket observer the government, it follows that government becomes an agent that can neither foresee nor influence the course of the market's movement. The New Keynesian school, discussed later in this chapter, has shown that government policy can influence market outcomes, despite rational expectations, when wages are "sticky." This, however, introduces institutional considerations – for example, wages will not be sticky in the absence of unions, long-term contracts, and other market "imperfections" – that change the preanalytical depiction of the economy characteristic of most rational expectation models.[17]

This conclusion of the rational expectations logic led to results of major significance. One is the so-called Policy-Ineffectiveness Proposition, according to which neither fiscal nor monetary policy, if anticipated, can exert any long-run real effects.[18] Expansionary fiscal policy, for example, will be offset over the long run by the rational response of increased saving in order to meet the inevitable increase in future tax liabilities.[19]

17. See Stanley Fischer, "Long-Term Contracts, Rational Expectations, and the Optimal Money Supply Rule," *Journal of Political Economy*, 85 (No. 1, February 1977): 191–205.
18. Robert E. Lucas, "Some International Evidence on Output–Inflation Trade-offs," *American Economic Review*, 63 (June 1973): 326–34, and Thomas Sargent and Neil Wallace, "Rational Expectations, the Optimal Monetary Instrument and the Optimal Money Supply Rule," *Journal of Political Economy*, 83 (April 1975): 241–55. The proposition does not follow strictly from the rational expectations hypothesis. However, it was with the use of the rational expectations hypothesis within the equilibrium approach that the proposition was discovered. See Bennet McCallum, "The Current State of the Policy Ineffectiveness Proposition," *American Economic Review*, 69 (May 1979): 240–5.
19. A second conclusion is the "Lucas critique," which states that the effect of policy changes cannot be evaluated insofar as the policy measures themselves change the parameters of estimation. This critique

As with the initial tautological character of the rational expectations hypothesis, the Policy-Ineffectiveness Proposition can be criticized as fatally flawed or simply as an unacceptable "view." The first interpretation, as we have seen, questions the depiction of market actors as possessing analytical skills or empirical information of the most trained econometricians.

A far more penetrative critique seems to us to focus on the nature of the self-guiding market as a metaphor for the larger universe to which the rational expectations hypothesis is directed as a heuristic. That larger universe, in turn, can be looked at from two perspectives. One of these examines capitalism as a social order, thereby bringing to the fore the specific social arrangements – including the market – that differentiate it from other orders such as feudalism, ancient hunting-and-gathering societies, and socialisms of whatever kind. This is an approach we shall explore in depth in our final chapters.

A second perspective focuses on the heuristic as an asocial representation of the market. The market then comes to resemble a wholly inanimate sequence of events whose constitutive units – including government – are robbed of volition or influence, and for that reason become completely predictable, save only for exogenous happenings. Human action is therefore lowered, or raised, to the same level as that of combustion, tensile strength, noise and other such phenomena of the physical world.

Is this approach useful? As with its tautological character, the contention cannot be empirically refuted. But at some deeper level, the application of a scientific construction of reality to social events goes against the grain. A central reason for this is the existential impossibility of excluding from

puts into question the large-scale Keynesian econometric models on which much macro forecasting is based. See Robert Lucas, "Economic Policy Evaluation: A Critique," in Karl Brunner and Allan Meltzer, eds., "The Philips Curve and Labor Markets," Supplement to the *Journal of Monetary Economics*, 1 (April 1976): 19–46.

social analysis the entirely human categories of purpose and will, not least as these are integrally connected with the concept of government. To declare that purpose and will are of no consequence in the unfolding of economic life is unacceptable in a fashion qualitatively different from their exclusion in the analysis of atomic or celestial events.

A less impassioned, but no less deep barrier to the universal applicability of the mode of natural science to the realm of social happenings is posed by the different conceptions of time in the two research objects. Time in logical and many physical processes is ergodic, or without intrinsic significance. Time in social processes is historic, or of constitutive importance. As Hicks writes: "Economics is in time, in a way that natural sciences are not. All economic data are dated; so that inductive evidence can never do more than establish a relation which appears to hold with the period to which the data refer." Paul Davidson, citing this passage, goes on to assert:

> Although the well-known poor forecasting performances of most large-scale econometric models is consistent with the Keynes–Shackle–Hicks view of the absence of ergodic [nonhistoric] processes for macroeconomics, most economists cling to the belief in the ergodicity of economic phenomena. To acknowledge that a nonergodic world is inextricably tied to crucial choices cannot be turned into a science on a par with the immutable laws of natural science.[20]

Thus the rational expectations construal of economic events gains the strength and suffers the weakness of narrowing the distance between natural scientific and social scientific approaches to human events. At the time of the development of the rational expectations hypothesis, the compression of the reach of social policy was much in keeping with the tenor of the times, and may have accounted for the

20. Paul Davidson, "Rational Expectations: A Fallacious Foundation for Studying Crucial Decisions in the Decision-Making Process," *Journal of Post Keynesian Economics*, 5 (No. 2, 1982–3): 193–4.

enthusiastic embrace of an essentially self-effacing view of economics as a Copernican undertaking. Certainly it helps explain the sharp division between its enthusiastic endorsement at levels of high academic theory and the rejection or indifference with which it was regarded by government, or business or academic research organizations like the Brookings Institution. At some subterranean level, rational expectations failed by itself to displace the Keynesian situation, not because it was not potentially useful, but for a more formidable reason. As an existential metaphor, it was not acceptable.

IV

The attack on Keynesian economics did not come in discrete stages. Monetarism had its devotees (and still has) long after rational expectations had claimed the attention of major theorists. In much the same fashion, the two remaining principal criticisms – New Classical economics and New Keynesian economics – cannot be precisely dated with respect to their entrances and should not be considered as successive stages of a search for an alternative paradigm.

New Classical economics has been called "the equilibrium approach to macroeconomics."[21] As such, its proponents accept the rational expectations hypothesis and assume efficiency in all markets: The appellation "Classical" derives from the assumption of instantaneous market clearing across the economy. The approach begins with the mathematical specification of an individual agent's objective function, which is considered "representative" for all individuals or firms. Macroeconomic outcomes can then be thought of as the aggregation of all such agents.

"The goal of the new classical revolution," according to Gregory Mankiw, "was to rebuild macroeconomics beginning with microeconomic primitives of preferences and

21. Bennett McCallum, "New Classical Macroeconomics: A Sympathetic Account," *Scandinavian Journal of Economics*, 91 (No. 2, 1989): 223.

technology."[22] It was thus an effort to return to the analytical framework of a Walrasian system in which the attainment of general equilibrium was guaranteed by explicit exclusion of the kinds of disturbances that might be introduced by adaptive expectations or by a need to allow for institutional impediments such as sticky wages. The positive goal of New Classical economics was to root macroeconomics in mathematically rigorous microfoundations with given preferences and technology, returning to the research program launched by Samuelson and others in the 1940s. By using only "natural" conditions (Mankiw's "primitives"), New Classical economists sought to construct models whose structure was immune to changes in policy – that is, beyond the Lucas critique.

A key contribution of New Classical theory lies in its reintroduction of the business cycle as a focal point of economic analysis. This departs from nineteenth-century classical analysis of trajectories of long-term growth, but reintroduces variations in the rates of employment and output that had been excluded in the early applications of rational expectations.

In the face of assumptions about instantaneous market clearing, New Classical theory must introduce a new key assumption of large random fluctuations in the rate of technological change. These in turn lead to fluctuations in the relative prices of goods, to which individuals rationally alter both their consumption and their labor supply responses. This "inter-temporal labor substitution" effectively creates cycles of output, but all such fluctuations represent efficient responses to the exogenous changes in technological capabilities.[23]

Once more it is necessary to consider both the analytical and the conceptual gains of this novel approach. The ana-

22. Gregory Mankiw, "A Quick Refresher Course in Macroeconomics," p. 1652.
23. For a detailed overview, see G. Stadler, "Real Business Cycles," *Journal of Economic Literature*, 332 (December 1994): 1750–83.

lytical critique has been the focus of a number of studies that have raised doubts about the role (and even existence) of significant intertemporal labor substitution and regular technological shocks.[24] In addition, the broad picture of economic history implied by the "real business cycle" model has been shown to be seriously at odds with the actual U.S. experience in the 1980s.[25] As before, however, one must not lose sight of the Copernican defense. Real business cycle theory is, like all New Classical economics, an attempt to ground economic dynamics in the "primitives" of technological constraints and rational individual behavior, a perspective from which monetary and market-clearing difficulties disappear. For all the powerful contrary evidence, there is no a priori reason why this perspective should not prove eventually to be as powerful an insight as the seemingly counterfactual and deeply counterintuitive heliocentric model of planetary motion.

There remain, however, the same grounds for doubt that earlier applied to the rational expectations hypothesis. The heliocentric model of planetary motion leaves out nothing that seems intrinsically constitutive of the planetary system itself. But this cannot be said of models, such as real business cycles, that omit the entanglement of government in the workings of a market system. The assumption that government is powerless to affect the dynamic properties of a mar-

24. On the question of labor substitution, see J. G. Altonji, "Intertemporal Labor Supply: Evidence from Micro Data," *Journal of Political Economy*, 94 (No. 3, part 2, June 1986): S176–S215; Lawrence Summers, "Some Skeptical Observations on Real Business Cycles," *Federal Reserve Bank of Minneapolis Review*, 10 (No. 4, Fall 1986): 23–7; Alan Blinder, "The Fall and Rise of Keynesian Economics," *Economic Record* (December 1988): 286. Regarding technological shocks, see Summers, "Some Skeptical Observations on Real Business Cycle Theory," and Bennett McCallum, "New Classical Macroeconomics: A Sympathetic Account," *Scandinavian Journal of Economics*, 91 (No. 2, 1989): 229.
25. See Gregory Mankiw, "Real Business Cycles: A New Keynesian Perspective," *Journal of Economic Perspectives*, 3 (No. 3, Summer 1989): 79–90.

ket system is tantamount to declaring that government can be considered as a neutral field – an empty space – within which market dynamics occur. This conclusion depends, of course, on the prior assumption that the rational behavior itself is unaffected by social and economic needs and pressures – the social equivalent of some cosmic constant.[26]

When one remembers the gamut of fiscal and monetary incentives and disincentives that bear on individual action, this assumption seems to fall of its own weight. For one thing, the intensity of the sentiments of the actors regarding the deployment of government's powers becomes incomprehensible. More deeply, the assumption ignores the undeniable fact that government, in all its forms, is the creation of social orders and not their God-given environment. All the counter-Keynesian thrusts that we have so far considered come up eventually against this objection, and none surmounts it because, to our mind, it is insurmountable.

V

The issue here is of sufficient importance to warrant further consideration. Underlying the conceptual foundations of the New Classicism is a denial of the sociality not only of governments but of all economic agents and the markets in which they interact. Individual preferences and technology are considered "natural" – that is, outside the workings of the economy itself – and thus any changes in them are also natural. They are taken as given to the economic problem. From a purely analytical perspective, this point of view seems self-contradictory. How can a monadic entity – the Robinson Crusoe concept of the individual – serve as the basis for a *social* inquiry? The self-contradictoriness is given recognition in virtually all neoclassical textbooks, where it is all the more striking for being unintentional. For what is the first act that these monadic agents perform in their tex-

26. Bennett McCallum, "New Classical Macroeconomics: A Sympathetic Account," p. 226.

tual existences? Is it not to allocate their incomes rationally, so as to maximize their individual utilities? The usual critiques now focus on the problematical terms "rational" and "utilities."[27] But the crucial issue is not here. It lies in the simple concept of "income." An income cannot be allocated until it has been received, presumably by payment from another "individual." The innocent depiction of the monadic individual unwittingly reveals the irreducible sociality of the concept, throwing into question the analytical validity of the basis on which the microfoundational model rests.[28] Thus in formalizing and placing the individual – the so-called representative agent – at the center of the analysis, the New Classicals have eliminated all those aspects of behavior that are social, such as power, commitment, and values. For all practical purposes, they have eliminated the individual him- or herself. An insistence on the sociality of agents implies a very different approach to economics.

Here the Copernican heliocentric versus the Ptolemaic Earth-centered conception of the planetary system serves us in more than a purely metaphorical way. What Copernicus offered was not merely a conception of the system that would ultimately provide more accurate measurements of planetary motion, but also a model that provided a more cogent conception of the relation of the central celestial object – the sun – to the motions of the bodies that moved across the heavens, than that which saw their orbits as circling the Earth. By analogy, the central problem of macroeconomics has been not only to describe the specific failures of the system, such as business cycles, but to relate these

27. See, for example, Alfred Eichner, "Why Economics Is Not Yet a Science," in Alfred Eichner, ed., *Why Economics Is Not Yet a Science* (Armonk, NY: M. E. Sharpe, 1987), pp. 205–41.
28. See Robert Heilbroner, *Behind the Veil of Economics* (New York: W. W. Norton, 1988), pp. 190–1. For an explicit critique of the use of the representative agent in macroeconomics, see Alan P. Kirman, "Whom or What Does the Representative Individual Represent," *Journal of Economic Perspectives*, 6 (No. 2, Spring 1992).

transmarket failures to the underlying structure and forces of a capitalist order.

This relationship can be conceptualized in two different ways. One of them locates its causational principle in interactions that originate in individual market behavior. It traces large-scale systemic failure to small-scale market clearing failure – minuscule in each individual case, but leading by a process of aggregation to disturbances capable of arresting or altering economic life on a transmarket and even transnational basis. Based on the knowledge of individual market behavior and misbehavior – knowledge common to everyone – this view might be compared to the psychological conviction with which the Ptolemaic vision commended itself to our commonsense view of the Earth as the center of the universe. In our present case, it calls for the surrender of the intuitive conception of the central importance of individual microeconomic activities in favor of much less intuitively familiar "supramarket" forces that exert their effect on our market behavior "behind our backs," through changes in aggregate incomes or price levels.

Such a conception brought problems of a kind that soon involved Keynesian theory in deep contradictions and difficulties. Central among them was the absence of any delineation of a "macro force" that could compare in scientific exactitude with that of the maximizing individual. In its absence there seemed to be no irreducible, and therefore essential entity on which a coherent and convincing theory could be built. Thus the first consideration in reviewing the tension between micro and macro determination serves strongly to support the position of the anti-Keynesians who have reacted against "animal spirits," "liquidity preference," "uncertainty," and other such disembodied strategic elements whose roots in individual action – and behind action, individual motivation – were never made clear. Much of the search for a new classical situation has been an attempt to remedy this shortcoming.

There is, however, a second consideration which bears differently on the vexing problem of the centrality and primal importance of the individual as the necessary basis for theory. It has two manifestations. The first is the necessity to accommodate the undeniable importance of lodging action in "agents" rather than in abstract entities, such as the infamous "forces of history." When General Motors raises the prices of its automobiles, who or what is the responsible agent? How can we fix responsibility for market behavior if a chain of command deprives us of the motivational clarity we seek?

Organized social action of any kind, public or private, presents difficult and important questions for the micro theorist, but these questions are not insoluble. A much more perplexing problem presents itself when we inquire into the "force" of micro behavior itself. Here the focus of attention is the discrete individual, endowed with the capabilities of intelligence, memory, and will. Such characteristics are not difficult to identify. The difficulties emerge only when we ask of that intelligence, memory, and will what we mean by designating it as "individual." Humans do not, and cannot, form intelligence, organize memories, or exercise will as isolated beings, entirely self-sufficient in their mental and psychological processes. The development of the human psyche, from the earliest moments of infancy on, takes place through the gradual ingestion and incorporation of the individual's surroundings, from its earliest familial influences through its exposure to innumerable influences of other individuals, directly or indirectly. Thus the concept of "the individual" – the analytical focus of so much conventional social science – appears most clearly in the form of a unique distillation of social influences. In Marx's profound words, the individual appears as "the ensemble of social relations," a "chaotic conception" unless we penetrate the facade of "the individual" to its social roots.[29]

29. Karl Marx, "Theses on Feurerbach: VI," in Robert Tucker, ed., *The Marx–Engels Reader* (New York: W. W. Norton, 1972). Originally pub-

From this perspective, the abstract "forces" of history that are so often used illegitimately as constituting an agencylike power appear as part of the information, rumor, contagions of moods, hopes, and apprehensions, that enter into and help shape the living behavior that remains, in the end, the only social means by which a market system can exercise its powers. From this viewpoint, "micro" and "macro" merge, in that microbehavior cannot be understood without taking cognizance of its social origins, and social forces remain empty abstractions unless they enter into the motivational concreteness of one or more individuals.

This accounting requires a different appreciation of the limits of "the individual" from the cautions raised earlier. What we speak of as the irreducible atom of action is revealed as an ambiguous rather than sharply delineated entity, and the line of demarcation between "individual" and "social" is revealed as a blurred interface rather than a razor-sharp division. It is not our purpose, in stressing this almost universally overlooked complexity of microeconomic "foundations," to assert that micro and macro heuristics are indistinguishable or make no difference. Quite the contrary, it is our intention to recognize that both perspectives have legitimacy, and that an exclusive reliance on one alone leads to a weaker rather than more robust framework for social explanation. That also implies that the touchstone of "scientificity," for which microfoundations have an obvious affinity, may not be the only criterion required to appraise the effort in social rather than natural terms; and that the achievement of Copernicus cannot be used as an exclusive metaphor for understandings that also require the concep-

lished in 1888. See also Robert Heilbroner, *Marxism: For and Against* (New York: W. W. Norton, 1980), pp. 46–7; On the relation between the Marxian conception of the individual and feminist and post-structuralist approaches, see William Milberg and Bruce Pietrykowski, "Objectivism, Relativism and the Importance of Rhetoric for Marxist Economics," *Review of Radical Political Economics*, 26 (No. 1, 1994): 85–109.

tual perspectives of Plato, Marx, Freud, and other such profoundly influential shapers of our social understanding.[30]

VI

It remains only to discuss a final alternative model: New Keynesian economics.[31] The model must be considered if for no other reason than that it does not reduce government to impotence by assumption, and by accepting the stickiness of wages and prices does not assume that markets clear automatically. This feature immediately rescues it from many of the criticisms that have been leveled against the New Classical theories.

What makes New Keynesian models "new" is that they are built on the explicit basis of behavior based on rational expectations and guided by the realization of all existing opportunities to maximize individual welfare. The models are therefore an effort to show that the original Keynesian outcomes of massive macro dysfunction can exist even in an economy in which Walrasian behavior is the norm, or, in other words, that maximizing behavior is not sufficient to produce Walrasian (or New Classical) outcomes if market imperfections are such as to prevent market clearing.

The explicit attention to market behavior therefore adds to New Keynesian theory a previously absent degree of concern with institutional rigidities that prevent market clearing. Originally focused solely on problems of labor contracts, these market imperfections have since widened to include the need to maintain "efficiency wages" – higher-than market wages to retain the efficiency of a trained work force – and "menu costs" imposed by the need to keep cus-

30. See Henry J. Aaron, "Public Policy, Policy Values, and Consciousness," *Journal of Economic Perspectives*, 8 (No. 2, Spring 1994), passim.
31. For a collection of some important New Keynesian articles, see Gregory Mankiw and David Romer, *The New Keynesian Economics* (Cambridge, MA: MIT Press, 1991), Vols. 1 and 2.

tomers fully informed as to altered price schedules, as well as by the presence of monopolistic competition, information asymmetries and "hysteresis" inherent to the dynamics of certain economic processes.[32]

This last school of thought must also be evaluated from the dual perspectives of analytics and vision. The criticisms of the analytics are similar in nature to those leveled against the New Classicals. Doubt has been expressed over the empirical significance of any of the specific New Keynesian contribution, although all things considered, New Keynesianism fares no worse on this level than any of its rivals.[33] The visionary assessment is more interesting, for New Keynesianism epitomizes the inward turn of economic thought of which we have already spoken. The research agenda is largely a response to the New Classical claim that involuntary unemployment is impossible in a free market economy composed entirely of rational consumers and firms. The New Keynesians have accepted the New Classical methodology of underpinning all theory with rational-choice mi-

32. The Mankiw and Romer volume cited in the previous footnote covers most of these topics. On monopolistic competition, see Olivier Blanchard and N. Kiyotaki, "Monopolistic Competition and the Effects of Aggregate Demand," *American Economic Review*, 77 (No. 4, September 1987): 647–66. Regarding efficiency wages and asymmetric information, see Bruce Greenwald and Joseph Stiglitz, "Imperfect Information, Credit Markets and Unemployment," *European Economic Review*, 31 (1978): 444–56. On hysteresis and unemployment, see Olivier Blanchard and Lawrence Summers, "Hysteresis and the European Unemployment Problem," *NBER Macroeconomics Annual* (1986): 15–78.
33. For example, there has been scant empirical evidence on whether menu costs are high enough to explain the persistently high rates of unemployment in advanced capitalist countries. By rooting all macroeconomic outcomes in the behavior of representative agents, the New Keynesians have ignored problems of heterogeneity of agents as well as the question of aggregation itself. Not surprisingly, the New Classical theorists have criticized the New Keynesians for relying too heavily on discredited Keynesian concepts such as the IS/LM model. See Robert G. King "Will the New Keynesian Macroeconomics Resurrect the IS-LM Model?" *Journal of Economic Perspectives*, 7 (No. 1, Winter 1993): 67–82.

crofoundations, but have sought to prove that with certain market imperfections present, involuntary unemployment may result. The New Keynesian project is thus a response to the New Classicals, not a research effort aimed at putting forth a new economic vision.

But perhaps the decisive identifying aspect of the school is its insistence that the proper scope of macroeconomic discussion is limited to the supply side. In a complete reversal of the traditional Keynesian perspective, demand factors are considered of secondary importance.[34] Such a view leads to a fundamental abandonment of Keynes's insight that a monetary economy, even with perfectly functioning markets, will be prone to unemployment due to insufficient effective demand. Paul Davidson thus appropriately characterized the New Keynesian position as "throwing out Keynes's baby with the New Classical Economics bathwater!"[35]

It is hardly surprising that the egregious weakness of New Keynesianism lies in the realm of policy. Having attributed involuntary unemployment to coordination failures and market imperfections rather than the failure of aggregate demand, many New Keynesian economists are silent on questions of macropolicy. Indeed, insofar as New Keynesians assert, contrary to the New Classicals, that market failures have a rational, supply-sided basis, policy has a much smaller role than it does for traditional Keynesians. Interest rate policy is out of bounds, along with fiscal demand man-

34. In his review of the "most important ideas and themes" of New Keynesianism, Gordon omits demand because demand issues "are not at the heart of the conflict between New-Keynesian and New-Classical macroeconomics." See Robert Gordon, "What Is New-Keynesian Economics," *Journal of Economic Literature*, 28 (September 1990): 1117. Efficiency wage theories of involuntary unemployment have been particularly vulnerable to the critique that they ignore the demand effects of wage changes. See, for example, Patrick Mason, "Variable Labor Effort, Involuntary Unemployment, and Effective Demand," *Journal of Post Keynesian Economics*, 15 (No. 3, Spring 1993): 427–42.

35. Paul Davidson, "Would Keynes be a New Keynesian?" *Eastern Economic Journal*, 18 (No. 4, Fall 1992): 450.

agement, since micro-incentives are the presumed source of economic movement. In terms of their policy views, it is difficult to distinguish New Keynesians from either monetarists or New Classicals. With their focus on atomistic agents interacting in individual markets, the policy concerns of New Keynesians revolve around the efficiency of resource allocation. A self-proclaimed New Keynesian, Alan Blinder admits that the New Keynesian ideas are important, "because economists like to rest the case for government intervention on externalities."[36] To put it differently, according to Mankiw and Romer, "Many of the traditional arguments *against* active stabilization policy . . . may remain valid even if one is persuaded by New Keynesian Economics."[37]

In sum, it is not too much to declare, along with Robert Gordon, that the apparent aim of the New Keynesian school is to "tease" out desired results from an initial position, rather than to devise creative policy departures to attain desired ends.[38] New Keynesian economics thereby comes more and more to resemble a game played with and against other economists, on whose outcome nothing much depends except academic prestige, rather than a serious undertaking that must be played out, for keeps, in the real world.

VII

It is time to review our argument. No successor to the Keynesian consensus has been found. Monetarism, rational expectations, New Classical and New Keynesian economics alike, have all sought to provide such a new point of intellectual agreement, but without success. Thus the single most

36. Alan Blinder, "The Fall and Rise of Keynesian Economics," p. 289.
37. Introduction to Mankiw and Romer, eds., *The New Keynesian Economics* (Cambridge, MA: MIT Press, 1991), Vols. 1 and 2, p. 3; emphasis added.
38. Robert Gordon, "What Is New-Keynesian Economics," *Journal of Economic Literature*, 28 (September 1990): 1115–71.

immediately apparent characteristic of the era since Keynesianism's decline is the dissonance and disarray that have superseded the unity and stability of the preceding classical situation. As we said at the outset, no such period of prolonged intellectual disagreement can be found in the history of economic thought.

Interestingly, the level of disagreement among mainstream macroeconomists can easily be overstated. Although New Classicals and New Keynesians are sometimes dramatically described as "arch-opposites," they have more in common than in conflict.[39] Both groups agree that macroeconomics must be rooted in the rational-choice microfoundations of all agents, and both share a skepticism with respect to the effectiveness of demand management as a means of overcoming inflation and unemployment. In a survey of 936 economists, Frey et al. found broad consensus on the view that "the price system is considered to be an effective and desirable social mechanism," but much less agreement on macro and monetary issues.[40]

The problem then is not that of internal disagreement, but of confusion and failure at the level of vision. For all its analytical brilliance, the retreat into rational choice has also revealed the absence of a conceptual center able to hold sway both within and outside the economics profession. Preanalytical shortcomings reflect the fragility of theories with respect to economic problem solving. Before turning, in the next chapter, to a discussion of the root causes of this visionary failure, we must first explore this crucial weakness.

The absence of a well-defined consensual core in modern economics has placed the burden of generating new ideas on the extremely malleable precepts of rational choice.

39. This term is taken from ibid.

40. Bruno Frey, Werner Pommerehne, Friederich Schneider, and Guy Gilbert, "Consensus and Dissension Among Economists: An Empirical Inquiry," *American Economic Review*, 74 (No. 5, December 1984): 986–94.

Such flexibility would be a strength if *empirical* inquiry could satisfactorily sort out the valid from the invalid insights of rational decision making. But that has not been the case. The econometric practices of the various rational-choice theoretics have encountered a barrage of criticisms, ranging from the recognition of the widespread use of "data mining," through the difficulty of replication of published empirical studies, and the problem of calibration and abuse of the rhetoric of "significance," to the fragility of the hypothesis-testing methodology itself. Econometrics has thereby attained a degree of indeterminacy akin to that of the theoretical edifice it is intended to support, with the result that analysis conducted in its name can be used to verify almost any hypothesis.[41] According to Lawrence Summers, "econometric results are rarely an important input to theory creation or the evolution of professional opinion generally."[42] The tenuous status of econometrics in generating economic knowledge has contributed to a change in the focus of theorizing, which no longer requires refutation but simply must be presented as "testable."[43]

41. On specification problems, see Edward E. Leamer, "Let's Take the Con out of Econometrics," *American Economic Review*, 73 (No. 1, March 1983): 31–43. On the problem of inference and data mining, see Steven Caudill, "Econometrics in Theory and Practice," *Eastern Economic Journal*, 16 (No. 3, July–September 1990): 249–56. Regarding the difficulty of replication, see William G. Dewald et al., "Replication in Empirical Economics: the *Journal of Money, Credit and Banking* Project," *American Economic Review*, 76 (No. 4, September 1986): 587–603. On the historical links between neoclassical economics and econometrics, see Philip Mirowski, "The Probabilistic Counterrevolution, or how Stochastic Concepts Came to Neoclassical Economic Theory," *Oxford Economic Papers*, 41 (1989): 217–35. For a discussion of the abuse of significance tests, see Donald M. McCloskey, *The Rhetoric of Economics* (Madison, WI: University of Wisconsin Press, 1985), Chapter 9.
42. Lawrence Summers, "The Scientific Illusion in Empirical Macroeconomics," *Scandinavian Journal of Economics*, 93 (No. 2, 1991): 129, 133.
43. Lawrence Boland, *The Methodology of Economic Model Building: Methodology After Samuelson* (New York: Routledge, 1989).

But the problem lies even deeper than this, and once again the notion of vision provides the key. The concept of a classical situation, as we have stressed, requires not only a certain extent of agreement among economists, but also a significant amount of confidence in its vision by those outside the profession. As we see it, noneconomists look for three such persuasive elements. First, economists are expected to provide a persuasive description of economic phenomena that makes sense of our current and past economic life-experience as individuals and communities. Our criticisms of the visionary status of the competing views to succeed the dethroned Keynesianism indicate that each view has been fundamentally deficient in this regard. The New Classical and New Keynesian visions insist on the primacy of the "natural" individual – that is, presocial and *given* to the economic problem. In the New Classical case, this requirement is taken to the extreme, with all outcomes perceived as natural and optimal. In the New Keynesian case, the effort to show Keynesian results using only rational-choice microfoundations suppresses the importance of the heterogeneity of agents and the problem of aggregation over these representative individuals.

Second, noneconomists seek guidance to the redress of specific economic problems. Here there has been a marked failure across all mainstream strains of thought. It lies in their common belief in the irrelevance – worse, the impotence – of "policy," which is to say the uselessness of political (governmental) powers to affect the outcome of economic dynamics. This attitude represents more than a distancing of economics from the disorderliness of politics or a frustration with the difficulties of applying "scientifically" exact economic remedies. It is an abdication from the moral obligations of a discipline that would have no raison d'être if social malfunctions did not exist in the portion of society we call "the economy."

To say as much is not to suggest that governmental interventions may not prove to be misguided, shortsighted, ineffectual, or even counterproductive. But to turn away from any attempts to lessen or even remove these malfunctions is to declare that Roosevelt's New Deal had no intended effect on the volume and distribution of incomes, that Eisenhower's Interstate Highway program did not succeed in improving the efficiency of the economy, or that the American entrance into two world wars was without foreseen consequences for the level of employment. To approach intervention with caution is very necessary, but to abjure it in a world of massive and persistent economic problems even in the wealthiest countries, and unspeakable squalor in much of the rest of the world, makes shameful the New Classical claim that all interventions are exercises in vain.

Third, one must consider that laissez-faire is also a policy choice, and that the tendency of economists to oppose state intervention of all sorts may be no more than an admission on their part that they simply don't know what to do. We are not the only observers to be struck by the moral irresponsibility of this withdrawal of economic concern from the hard realities of political life. Lawrence Summers concludes a scathing appraisal of the "scientific illusion" in modern macroeconomics with the words: "In the end I am not sure these theoretical exercises teach us anything at all about the world we live in."[44] In much the same vein of skeptical disbelief, Gregory Mankiw describes real business cycle theory as "potentially dangerous" in that "those who advise policy makers might . . . conclude that macroeconomic policies are unnecessary."[45]

44. Lawrence Summers, "The Scientific Illusion in Empirical Macroeconomics," pp. 144–5.
45. Gregory Mankiw, "Real Business Cycles: A New-Keynesian Perspective," *Journal of Economic Perspectives*, 3 (No. 3, Summer 1989): 79.

In our view, this retreat of modern economic theory from the policy arena is the single most important result of the crisis of vision in the discipline since Keynesianism was driven from center stage. It is time to turn to the questions that this belief asks: How can one explain such a failure of nerve? What can one suggest as a possible remedy? These are the daunting matters to which we now direct our attention.

CHAPTER 6

THE NATURE OF SOCIETY

I

In our previous chapter we have followed the development of macroeconomic thought during recent years, stressing its analytical successes and visionary failures. Now it is time to reflect on the larger problem of our study – not to trace or criticize in detail the course of economics since the disappearance of the Keynesian classical situation, but to clarify the strategic roles played by both vision and analysis in that unstable and, in our view, essentially retrogressive period. In this task, the contemporary theoretical disarray is as important for its illustrative as for its substantive content. We cannot know what will be the outcome of the present state of affairs, although in our next chapter we shall venture a few suggestions about the requirements for a new theoretical foundation. But first there remains the necessary task of reviewing, summarizing, and generalizing about the roles of vision and analysis in the task of economic theorizing itself.

Let us begin by posing a question that we have already noted, but have not yet pursued to its roots. Why is it that none of the theoretical departures since Keynesianism took hold? To generalize about the larger issues of vision and analysis, we must surely have in mind some plausible answer to a question as seemingly simple as this.

One possible answer suggests itself immediately. It is that no alternative vision of sufficient persuasive power came to the fore. Kuhn argues that no paradigm is ever overthrown except by a viable successor. The argument smacks of circularity, but it has enough empirical appeal to warrant some consideration. Who were the contenders for the place left empty by the decline of Keynesian theory? In Cambridge, England, a "Post Keynesian" school waged intellectual war with Cambridge, Massachusetts, over the internal consistency of the neoclassical theory of capital and the aggregate production function, but the victory of the English side led to nothing like a substantial reformulation of Keynesian (or general) economic theory. In retrospect, it was a tempest in a teapot.[1] Furthermore, the tempest remained within the teapot because despite their impressive analytics, the contestants did not have a comprehensive vision of what a new classical situation might be. To this day there is little agreement on what constitutes Post Keynesianism. And the effort has been further hampered by the conflict between those Post Keynesians who stress the role of money and uncertainty, and those who emphasize nonmonetary production relations.[2]

1. It is not surprising that the aggregate production function has resurfaced in neoclassical circles (e.g. in the new growth theory and New Classicism generally), since that group includes those who have retained Ferguson's "faith," despite the criticisms; see C. E. Ferguson, *The Neoclassical Theory of Production and Distribution* (Cambridge University Press, 1969), p. xvii. But the Cambridge controversy appears also to have failed to convince many Marxist, neo-Marxist, Regulation School, and Institutionalist economists.
2. On the irreconcilability of the various Post Keynesian approaches, see Geoffrey Harcourt and Omar Hamouda, "Post Keynesian Economics: Quite Old or Something New?" in John Pheby, ed., *New Directions in Post Keynesian Economics* (Aldershot, NY: Edward Elgar, 1989), pp. 1–24. Prominent Post-Keynesian economists stressing money and uncertainty include G. L. S. Shackle, *Epistemics and Economics* (Cambridge University Press, 1972); Paul Davidson, *Money and the Real World* (New York: John Wiley & Sons, 1982); and Hyman Minsky, *Stabilizing an Unstable Economy* (New Haven: Yale University Press, 1986). Those stressing "real" production conditions include Luigi Pasinetti, *Lectures on the Theory of Production* (New York: Columbia University Press, 1977); Ian Steedman, *Trade Amongst Growing Economies* (Cambridge University Press, 1979); and Heinz Kurz and Neri Salvadori, *Theory of Production* (Cambridge University Press, 1995). Those who have developed the approach of Michal Kalecki are also considered to be in the Post-Keynesian camp. See Malcolm C. Sawyer, *The Economics of Michal Kalecki* (Armonk, NY: M. E. Sharpe,

Two other "outside" contenders also proved unable to provide the basis for a new consensual base for economics. One of these was Marxism, which, we tend to forget, had maintained a recognizable identity across a century of intellectual history, an achievement without equal in the narrative of economic thought. But Marxism was unable to provide such a launching pad for numerous reasons. One of them, of course, was the arguable but unavoidable association of theoretical Marxism with Soviet reality. A second reason was the hostility of American, and to a lesser extent European, academic sentiment to the radical views that were properly associated with Marxian analysis. Yet a third was a division within the Marxist camp into a number of antagonistic schools, along with a "fundamentalist" Marxian approach. For all these reasons, nothing resembling a widely held Marxian view entered the lists, and given the obstacles we have mentioned, it is doubtful that it would have attracted a large following, had it done so.[3]

Meanwhile, yet another possible contender, Institutionalism, also failed to put forward a corpus of thought of sufficient unity to become the new center of theoretical work. A newly founded *Journal of Economic Issues* became the ve-

1985). It is important to note that Alfred Eichner's effort to build a coherent amalgam of these views has been largely ignored. See Alfred Eichner, *The Macrodynamics of Advanced Market Economies* (Armonk, NY: M. E. Sharpe, 1992).

3. The different strains of American Marxism include the monopoly capital view, best known in the writings of Paul Baran and Paul Sweezy; see, for example, their classic, *Monopoly Capital* (New York: Monthly Review Press, 1966), as well as the journal *Monthly Review*; the Social Structure of Accumulation group founded by Samuel Bowles, David Gordon and Thomas Weisskopf (see for example, their *After the Wasteland* (Armonk, NY: M. E. Sharpe, 1991); the analytical Marxists [e.g., Jon Elster, *Making Sense of Marx* (Cambridge University Press, 1985)], the overdetermination Marxists [e.g., Steven Resnick and Richard Wolff, *Knowledge and Class: A Marxian Critique of Political Economy* (Chicago: University of Chicago Press, 1987)], and the fundamentalist Marxists [e.g., Anwar Shaikh, "Political Economy and Capitalism: Notes on Dobb's Theory of Crisis," *Cambridge Journal of Economics*, 2 (June 1979): 233–51].

hicle for numerous institutionally based critiques and formulations, building on the contributions of Veblen and Ayres, but none was sufficiently influential to found a "school." Among these certainly the best known was the work of John Kenneth Galbraith, especially his successive books on *American Capitalism* (1952), *The Affluent Society* (1958), and *The New Industrial State* (1967). Although widely read and much discussed in the public prints, the work was never taken seriously by the academic world, whether because its analytical apparatus was insufficiently developed, or because its vision – somewhat like that of Veblen – was difficult to codify as a series of positive, rather than critical statements.

It is important to add that the failure of any of these alternative approaches to attain the dominance necessary to constitute a new classical situation is partly due to the rigid and hierarchical organization of the economics profession. Those who hold positions at the few "top" universities carry a disproportionate amount of power over hiring, publishing, and the granting of research funds, including federal government research funding through the National Science Foundation. The hiring of new economists by the leading universities is limited to those trained at only a few select graduate programs. And the major academic journals are equally dominated by articles written by economists from those same schools. Graduates of only seven departments accounted for 54%, 58%, and 74% of articles published in the *American Economic Review,* the *Journal of Political Economy,* and the *Quarterly Journal of Economics,* respectively, for the years 1973–8.[4] Within such a structure, the possibilities for a fundamental change in the direction of thinking are obviously limited.

4. E. Ray Canterbery and Robert Burkhardt, "What Do We Mean by Asking If Economics Is a Science?" in Alfred Eichner, ed., *Why Economics Is Not Yet a Science* (Armonk, NY: M. E. Sharpe, 1983): 15–40.

II

In the absence of a new commanding vision from without, academic economic thought turned within, a development that emerged spontaneously among all the theoreticians we discussed in our previous chapter. As we know, this inward movement took the form of an enlargement of the role of analysis to the point where it not only obscured the absence of a new commanding vision, but served, in large degree, as a substitute for it. Thomas Mayer describes this retreat as an obsession with "precision" to the neglect of "truth," where the latter is broadly conceived as a plausible and persuasive explanation of economic phenomena. To Mayer, contemporary economic theory has been ruled by "the principle of the strongest link," which allocates research toward that aspect of the problem in which advance is most easily gained, and which ascribes to the entire argument the strength of this particular aspect, to the neglect of the robustness of the model as a whole.[5]

A number of economists have noted this growing obsession with analytical sophistication. Already in 1975, Robert A. Gordon, in his presidential address to the American Economic Association, warned economists of the danger of placing "rigor" ahead of "relevance."[6] But such early warnings were not heeded. Alan Blinder writes:

> The rational expectations revolution was a godsend for aspiring young technicians. It not only pushed macrotheory in more abstract and mathematical directions, but brought in its wake a new style of econometrics that was far more technically demanding than the old methods it sought to replace.[7]

5. Thomas Mayer, *Truth Versus Precision in Economics* (Aldershot, NY: Edward Elgar, 1993).
6. Robert A. Gordon, "Rigor and Relevance in a Changing Institutional Setting," *American Economic Review*, 66 (March 1976).
7. Alan Blinder, "The Fall and Rise of Keynesian Economics," *Economic Record*, 64 (December 1988): 283–4.

A confirming judgment can be found in a recent survey of graduate students in the top U.S. economics departments.[8] By a very large majority, students welcomed the technical challenge of the "new" economics. Sixty-eight percent believed that a thorough knowledge about the economy itself was unimportant for the attainment of success in the economics profession. Only three percent believed it was very important. Thus, as we search for reasons why the efforts of the last two decades have failed to establish a new compelling center of vision for economics, "the lure of technique" must be added to the failure of nonmainstream approaches to provide a new visionary inspiration.

The rise of a conservative cast to American politics, during the Reagan and Bush presidencies, may also have played a role: Blinder specifically attributes the rise of New Classical economics, with its central thesis of governmental impotence, to this general political trend of affairs. He notes that the new economics never caught on in Europe, where the political climate remained more centrist:

> The relative strengths of conservative and liberal ideology obviously vary both over time and through space. My argument is that [anti-Keynesian] new classical theory could have attracted a large following only in a country and at a time when right-wing ideology was on the ascendancy, as was true in the United States in the 1970s and 1980s.[9]

III

There are, in other words, a number of possible explanations for the failure of any single theory to take the place of dethroned Keynesianism; and indeed, the phenomenon itself may perhaps be best understood as multicausal. Nonetheless there remain two explanations that seem to us of a much less suppositious character. The first of these is the growing

8. David Colander and Arjo Klamer, "The Making of an Economist" *Journal of Economic Perspectives*, 1 (No. 2, Fall 1987).
9. Blinder, "The Fall and Rise of Keynesian Economics," 285.

emphasis on the "scientific" status of economics, with a closely allied tendency to subsume economic phenomena under the aegis of natural law. The second, related to the first, is the inability of modern economics to come to terms with, or even to speak of capitalism as the social order to whose specific workings economics directs its analytical attention, and from which it derives its political and social vision.

The effort to establish economics as a scientific endeavor, rightfully to be considered at least potentially on a par with that of science, has a long history within the development of economic thought. A more or less explicit emulation of "natural" mechanisms can be seen in such otherwise differing works as those of Smith, Ricardo, or Marx, all of them searching for impersonal, suprasocial forces that imposed an objective necessity over the wills of the actors who operated within the economic, as contrasted with moral or social or political, realm. Neoclassical theory, likewise, has always welcomed the lawlike underpinnings of marginalism, with its exogenous and thus "natural" basis in individual preferences and endowments of wealth and technology. In all these depictions, from the Newtonian perspective of the classicals to the energy-conservation view of the early neoclassicals, the economy resembles a great machine, governed by strict and mathematically describable laws of motion. Economic outcomes thus become grounded in processes that can be viewed as counterparts of those that regulate the configurations and movements of the heavens above and the earth below. Nature and society in this way approach each other conceptually.[10]

10. William Milberg discusses this thesis with a focus on Ricardo and Walras in his "Natural Order and Postmodernism in Economic Thought," *Social Research*, 60 (No. 2, Summer 1993): 255–77. For a detailed and highly original treatment of the various failed efforts at naturalism in neoclassical thought and their distinction from the Newtonianism of the classicals, see Philip Mirowski, *More Heat than Light: Economics as Social Physics, Physics as Nature's Economics* (Cambridge University Press, 1989).

From this viewpoint, that which makes the Keynesian classical situation so interesting to a historian of economic thought is its sharp break from this prevailing conception. As we have seen, the central role accorded to uncertainty, to "animal spirits," and to the irrationalities of choice in the capital markets establishes a gap between Keynes's vision of the social world and that which had prevailed before. In retrospect, the heretical, and ultimately indigestible aspect of Keynes's work may not have been its emphasis on large-scale malfunction, but his ascription of malfunction to social rather than mechanistic causes. Effective demand shortfalls, which reflect Keynesian uncertainties, are more likely to be important than resource scarcities, which arise out of mismatches of well-behaved supply and demand curves. So too, in the Keynesian treatment of accumulation, as we find it, for example, in the work of Joan Robinson, where technical change and factor mobility can overcome natural constraints: "Where this process [capital accumulation] confronts a natural barrier such as the scarcity of fertile land or labor, this natural barrier must give way rather than accumulation."[11]

The final demise of Keynesian hegemony was signaled by the resurgence of natural law conceptions of economic inquiry. Certainly the idea of rational expectations, which banished such hopelessly unscientific Keynesian conceptions as the "popularity contest" view of financial investment, the unpredictable location of the liquidity threshold, or even the notion of adaptive expectations implied by the IS/LM model, represented a reassertion of the natural law analogy. New Classical and New Keynesian premises likewise moved the vision of the economic process closer to a natural conception. New Classical theory removed the unpredictable influences of money – always a threat to such a conception,

11. Nina Shapiro, "The Revolutionary Character of Post-Keynesian Economics," *Journal of Economic Issues*, 11 (No. 3, September 1977): 552.

in that money is inexpungeably social in origin – and located "economic" dynamics, such as the business cycle, in the natural forces of technology or individual preference shifts. New Keynesian theorists have followed the New Classicals in the assertion of the primacy of individual optimization in determining macroeconomic outcomes.

Thus a central tendency visible since the demise of Keynesianism has been a more or less explicit desire to return to the tradition of economics as an inquiry in which the fundamental driving forces could be as clearly identified as in the classical models of Smith and Ricardo. This search for a natural law focus has had a double consequence. On the one hand, as we have emphasized, it brought to economics the deterministic clarity it sought and the status associated with the most prestigious branch of human inquiry.[12] On the other hand, its deliberate identification with science prevented economics from explicitly grounding itself in the contingent historical and political requirements of the prevailing social order. To the extent that market actors and technology are "given" to the economic problem, economics has little ability to explain market outcomes. In this sense, contemporary economics *explains* nothing. Only if markets are viewed not simply as resource allocation machines, but as social constructs that serve a social function, will the role of organizational structure, technological innovations, and cultural norms and habits be integrated more centrally into economic analysis. This brings us at last to a direct confrontation with a source of intellectual disquiet to which we have only made passing reference until now. It is the relation between economics as a mode of vision and analysis, and the needs and problems of the social order in which it is embedded; namely, capitalism.

12. This was not all gain, for the increasing need for scientificity has had to contend with a growing insecurity of the scientific paradigm itself, especially in its "positivist" form. See Deborah Redman, *Economics and the Philosophy of Science* (New York: Oxford University Press, 1993).

IV

Capitalism is a complex system of social and political relations that collectively determine the dynamics of its economic institutions. The system displays considerable variations, both from era to era, and from nation to nation within each era, but we believe that the three characteristics below are common to all, and serve to highlight that which is essential for our purposes:[13]

Capital Accumulation. The first consideration for capitalism, as for all social orders, is political, which is to say the pursuit of the end on which its dominant class depends for power and prestige. In older imperial orders, this was the enlargement of territory or the subjugation of competitive centers of territorial power. For capitalism it is the accumulation of capital. This requires a few words of explication concerning the difference between capital and wealth, perhaps unnecessary, but too important to omit. Wealth is perhaps best conceived as a natural or manmade object (a herd of cattle, a hoard of gold) whose importance lies in the power or prestige it confers upon its owner. Like wealth, capital is a symbol of power and prestige, but unlike wealth it cannot be passive – that is, used only for show, or great reward. On the contrary, the typical use of wealth-as-capital is to set into motion activities for which wealth would never be disbursed. Specifically, capital takes on a protean and dynamic form as its owners use it to buy such common objects as cloth and labor power, which are then combined to create commodities offered for sale for more than they cost. This process takes place not once, but again and again, in pursuit of the end of increasing its value. Here we have Marx's famous circuit M-C-M′, a self-expanding process that would threaten the very existence of wealth, but that infuses capital with life.

13. See Robert Heilbroner, "The Nature of Economics," *Challenge* (Jan.–Feb. 1995): 20–6.

Two aspects of this process are germane to our present concerns. The first is that it is the cause for such familiar aspects of capitalism as its continuous search for innovation, its aggressive strategies of offense, and stubborn strategies of self-protection – all comprehensible only as means by which its units of capital (the "firms" of modern day society) respond to the imperative of a social order in which the failure to expand capital means absorption by a more successful firm. More importantly, because less widely recognized, it is that the drive for capital can be understood only as a sociopolitical, not an "economic" end. Economics is concerned with allocations and choices, not with limitless accumulations of power and prestige. Hence such conventional economic conceptions as rational choice or diminishing marginal utility may apply to the small-scale determinations of day-to-day strategies, but have little or no relevance to the central process of capitalism itself – a process of accumulation, comprehensible only as a manifestation of the suprarational ends of power and prestige that animate every stratified social order.

Market Allocation. The second distinctive characteristic of capitalism is organizational rather than sociopolitical. It is the coordination of production and the regulation of distribution by the largely unregulated competitive striving for advantageous purchase or sale called "the market." Such a regulatory or allocational determination is elsewhere left to the hand of tradition or assigned by the rod of command.

This unique "mechanism" not only bestows order on the drive for capital (termed *investment*), but is responsible as well for overseeing the provisioning of all members of the social order (called *consumption*). Because this means of coordination is so visible, so vital, and so animated, capitalism is often referred to as a "market system," but the designation is seriously deficient insofar as it ignores the underlying sociopolitical origins of the activities that the market must coordinate and guide, and the wide variation in the nature and scope of markets in particular cases. Markets are a necessary adjunct to an order built on capital accumulation, but they are not sufficient to constitute such a system.

Dual Realms. Last and by no means least, a capitalist order has a unique administrative form in its division into a "private" and a "public" realm. The latter is the repository of the powers found in every stratified social order: the promulgation and enforcement of law, the support of the general prerogatives of the dominant class, and the defense of the territory of the nation. In contrast, the private sector refers mainly to "economic" activities that in other orders remain within the aegis of tradition and/or command. Here we find not only the "mechanism" of the market, but the internal organization of the labor process, also largely exempt from political responsibility. Capitalist employers must obey the law established by the public realm, and cannot usurp its prerogatives, such as legal punishment. Otherwise, within wide limits they conduct their affairs as they wish, subject only to the "approval" of the market.

This bifurcation of realms not only vastly enhances the dynamic properties of capitalism but also sets the stage for the tense relationship between the two sectors that poses a constant problem for the design of effective economic policy. At the same time, large-scale exclusion of government power from the private sector undoubtedly discourages its use elsewhere. To that extent, capitalism is undoubtedly more hospitable to democracy and to the development of civil society than any nonbifurcated stratified system.

A final word: Three institutional characteristics – one sociopolitical (the accumulation drive), one organizational (the market), and one administrative (the coexistence of public and private realms) – set capitalism apart from all other social formations to date. All three characteristics mutually reinforce one another, and capitalism would not be workable in the absence of any. But if one considers the social formation as a whole, its historical place and influence surely derive mainly from the expansion process that remains at its core, a sociopolitical base that economics ignores at its peril.

This attempt to sketch out an ideal-typical framework of capitalism is not meant to suggest that variations in its forms cannot significantly alter its dynamics, or the character of the social and political life among various national capitalisms.[14] In this regard, one need only conjure up the ideal types suggested by "Dickensian" and "Swedish," or nineteenth-century American and twentieth-century Japanese capitalisms. Our point is therefore not to present a bill of particulars that could easily be faulted. It is rather to insist that some generalizing description, resembling that above, can represent with sufficient accuracy an ideal-typical capitalist mode, much as is the case with primitive social formations, so-called "tributary" systems, feudalisms, and perhaps centrally planned socialisms. The fundamental assertion, in other words, is that a recognizable form of "capitalist" socioeconomic organization can be identified in history. On this assertion rests the crucial argument to follow.

V

The argument claims that economics is a form of social inquiry peculiar to capitalist societies. The crisis of vision in the major recent economic developments is the failure even to acknowledge, much less to explore, this inextricable link. To deny it is drastically to reduce the effectiveness of economic thought as a tool for understanding society. To use representative agent rational choice as the organizing principle for thinking about modern organized capitalism not

14. On the perils of viewing capitalism as a monolith and the possibilities in a more historically and geographically contingent perspective, see the excellent essay by J. K. Gibson-Graham, "Waiting for the Revolution, or How to Smash Capitalism while Working at Home in Your Spare Time," *Rethinking Marxism*, 6 (No. 2, Summer 1993): 10–24. See also Michael Mann, *The Social Sources of Power* (Cambridge University Press, 1986).

only limits the scope of economics, but skews it in a direction that is incapable of providing a compelling explanation of our experience.

Here it may be useful to start our discussion by considering a contrary point of view put forward by the distinguished economist Jack Hirshleifer. Hirshleifer writes:

> It is ultimately impossible to carve off a distinct territory for economics, bordering on, but separated from other social disciplines. Economics penetrates them all, and is reciprocally penetrated by them. *There is only one social science.* What gives economics its imperialist invasive power is that our analytical categories – scarcity, cost, preferences, opportunities, etc. – are truly universal in application. Even more important is our structured organization of these concepts into the distinct yet intertwined processes of optimization on the individual decision level and equilibrium on the social level. Thus economics does really constitute the universal grammar of social science.[15]

Such a view would not find the intimate relation between economics and capitalism that we wish to stress. As a "universal grammar," economics would be discoverable in all social systems – not as "science," but as the expression of universal social categories such as production and distribution, or "scarcity, cost, preference," and the like. Hirshleifer's view might or might not claim that capitalism is a distinct historical entity recognizable, let us say, by its legal or property systems, but he clearly denies that "economics" bears an inextricable relationship to whatever legal or property system might impart such a distinct historical form to any social order.

Our own view takes another tack. It is no doubt possible to discover scarcity, cost, etc., in all social orders, although they may be differently denominated, as for example the "cost" of labor in a slave, a feudal, and a capitalist order. Unquestion-

15. Jack Hirshleifer, "The Expanding Domain of Economics," *American Economic Review*, 75 (No. 6, December 1985): 53.

ably, human attitudes such as "preferences" can also be discovered everywhere, insofar as it seems to be an aspect of "human nature" not to be indifferent to available options. And certainly all societies must produce and distribute their means of subsistence and/or glory. But we would claim that this universal grammar does not communicate a message of any economic interest or significance, unless it applies to a society that possesses the institutional and cultural elements of capitalism: indeed, the very meaning of "economic" would be unintelligible outside capitalism.

To make the point by concrete example, let us imagine ourselves examining an unfamiliar, but clearly noncapitalist social order, such as that of ancient Egypt, or the Kalahari bushpeople, or the former Soviet Union.[16] What knowledge would we need to understand the bonds that held the society together, the imperatives that moved it, the principles that governed its social structure, and above all, the causes that determined the historical path that it followed? A long list of candidates presents itself – anthropology, sociology, politics, psychology, history. But economics? If we knew all there was to know about the ancient Egyptians, the Kalahari, the Russians from the viewpoints of the disciplines we have mentioned, what is left for the study of economics to add? What does marginal utility or maximization tell us about scarcity, cost, preferences, and opportunities that will not be explained by psychology, sociology, politics, and the rest?

Let us now turn the question around. Assume that as members of such a noncapitalist culture we come to examine the United States, or Sweden or Japan, with the same purpose in mind. Will the span of studies from psychology through political "science" tell us why all these countries develop their productive capacities so unevenly across space and over time, why they are so often characterized by large numbers of individuals who cannot find work al-

16. This example is adapted from Robert Heilbroner, *Twenty-First Century Capitalism* (New York: W. W. Norton, 1993), pp. 22–5.

though there are crying needs to be met? It will not. We need an understanding of the categories and institutions we have listed above as a stylized description of capitalism, above all, its vital core of capital accumulation. That is to say, we need a conceptual vocabulary and an analytical repertoire that would be unavailable except through a discipline that devotes itself to the self-generated tendencies that we find only in capitalism. That discipline is economics.

The point warrants an additional word. We might indeed discover in a study of ancient Rome that the material progress of the empire displayed an uneven pattern over space and time, and that large numbers of would-be workers were without work. But in this case we know where to turn for clarification. It lies in the political mismanagement of state affairs. It does not lie in the spontaneous manifestations of a self-adjusting "economy" because there is no such thing. Production and distribution are largely guided by tradition or supervised by the state. There are street markets, and even a rudimentary "stock market," but there is no ubiquitous institutionalized process in which expansion-minded "businesses" vie for success by largely unhampered mutual rivalry.

We hasten to add, as well, that there is more than one vocabulary and repertoire of economics, so that the location and changeful pace of industry, or the spectacle of unemployment will look very different through lenses ground with a Marxian prescription and those ground to the order of a New Classical economist. But without some form of "economics" there would be no comprehension whatsoever of what we see. Psychology, sociology, and politics do not include unemployment or uneven growth in their conceptual or analytical concerns. That is to say that there exist aspects of a capitalist order that cannot be grasped without economics; or to turn the matter around, it is to say that economics cannot be learned or used without speaking of capitalism.

VI

This inextricable entanglement of economics with capitalism appears to be the best guarded secret of the profession. Indeed, one suspects that the secret is not even known to all economists. Oddly, the only schools of economics that openly declare the intimate relation between capitalism and economics are Marxian, institutional, and other "left" approaches; and Hayekian, von Misean, and related libertarian "right" approaches. In the great middle range that encompasses the majority of the theorizing we have been concerned with, there is virtually no mention of the problem at all.

It will, by now, come as no surprise that we consider this studied – or worse, innocent – failure to connect theory and historical contingency as lying at the heart of the inability of contemporary theory to constitute a new classical situation. The failure of mainstream economics to recognize the insistent presence of this underlying social order, with its class structure, its socially determined imperatives, its technologies and organizations, and its privileges and rights, derives from its preconceptual basis in a natural rather than a social construal of economic society. Such a preanalytic perspective, devoid of all the elements that connect economic life to a social matrix, cannot generate the resonances necessary for a fruitful vision. To say that for certain problems one takes the existence of capitalism as given and for others one does not, and thus that there is a division of labor among economists in which some economists do and some do not need to consider the broader social context, misses the point of the vision/analysis distinction. Depending on the vision, the very categories of analysis either encompass or ignore the broader social forces.[17]

17. Thus the vision/analysis distinction should not be reduced to that of content and form. See Donald McCloskey, *Knowledge and Persuasion in Economics* (Cambridge University Press, 1994).

It is certainly the case that earlier economists wove elements of a natural order into their visions. We find an invisible hand in Smith, a "natural" course of income distribution in Ricardo, self-engendered contradictions in Marx, a pervasive attainment of "progress" in the case of Mill, "biological" analogies for Marshall, and "propensities" to consume and save in Keynes. But these natural tendencies and forces were intimately connected with the social realities of a clearly perceived sociohistorical kind. Smith dealt at length with the institutional and motivational properties of a nascent capitalism; Ricardo largely ignored, but never denied the social realities of the capitalist scenario; Marx was continually at work exposing the social causalities behind seemingly "natural" events; Mill strongly believed that society could morally reorder its material framework; Marshall was a believer in the possibility of economic "chivalry," hardly a natural concept; and Keynes's monetary production economy was firmly connected with the depression era of the 1930s. No ideas of this kind becloud the rarefied world of contemporary economic theory. In our view, this divorce between social vision and technical analysis has been the great impediment to the formation of a new theoretical center.

The depoliticization of economics of course serves an ideological function, using the term not merely to mean biased discourse, but any discourse that claims universality.[18] Such an economics knows no historic specificity. Its vision and analysis are both without historical placement. They are absolutes, "above" the contingency that modifies all avowedly social constructs. A few examples, drawing on our foregoing sketch of capitalism will make the point. From a dehistoricized viewpoint, the idea of capital is that of any instrument of production, in no way different in status from the complementary instrument of labor, save that it is accorded the right to claim the value of any residual output that remains

18. Catherine Belsey, *Critical Practice* (London: Methuen, 1980), p. 5.

after payment of the market-determined incomes of all other factors, and of a portion (interest) due to itself. In a society that was historically static there would be little political significance in such an arrangement, but in one posited on the continuous pursuit of accumulation, that neutrality can hardly be claimed. In similar fashion, the concept of a general equilibrium as the configuration to which a "pure" capitalist economy naturally gravitates also appears to be a perfectly apolitical assumption, until recognition is accorded to the drive for technological and organizational innovation that reflects the capitalist "rage for accumulation." From such a perspective, general equilibrium appears as a concept that clashes directly with the sociopolitical requirements for a well-functioning capitalist regime.[19]

These criticisms are often voiced by economists of the left. But the failure of the contemporary vision goes beyond the well-established critique of "bourgeois economics." This failure manifests itself most clearly when even the dominant groups in society question the explanatory power of the reigning paradigm. Such ineffectiveness has become increasingly apparent since the crisis of Keynesianism. For the Keynesian classical situation, we can now appreciate more clearly than before, was based on a vision whose central message was not so much the endemic dysfunctionality of the capitalist order – that has an ancestry dating at least to Marx and before him to Malthus – but the ensuing conclusion that the use of government powers of demand management would be the only remedy capable of setting the disorder to right. This may have been a distasteful message for capitalism, but it was clearly not one that could be ignored.

By way of contrast, the visionary basis of contemporary economic thought has been the opposite, an affirmation of

19. Neoclassical general equilibrium theory is thus equally "relevant" to a perfectly planned socialist system. See Oskar Lange and Fred M. Taylor, *On the Economic Theory of Socialism* (New York: McGraw-Hill, 1938).

the reliability of rationally guided individual behavior as a sufficient condition for systemic order and prosperity. This is a very welcome message, but its ahistoricity undermines its usefulness as a new classical situation. Even the New Keynesian project, which identifies market failure as the cause of economic malfunction, is ultimately an endorsement of this view, since removal of market failures would, for the New Keynesians, overcome the malfunction. Gradually the vision conveyed by the "new" economics has moved from ideology to apologism – that is, from the expression, knowingly or otherwise, of unassailable political and social heuristics and aperçus to views that seem quite impossible to square with firsthand knowledge and historical research. For example, Blinder quotes Lucas: "To explain why people allocate time to unemployment we need to [know] why they prefer it to all other activities," and comments: "In Lucas's view, a person laid off from a job can, presumably, shine shoes in a railroad station or sell apples on street corners. If he is not doing any of these things, he must be *choosing* not to do so."[20] Not only can Robinson Crusoe never be involuntarily unemployed, but the Walrasian prereconciliation of diverse individual interests removes from analysis any semblance of a market, an institution integral to any capitalist system. The irony is that the order which such apologism serves is capitalism, the mention of which is taboo in modern economics.

After so much criticism, there is need for a last word, already anticipated in the opening words of this study. The lack of a viable classical situation was already a disturbing fact during the years in which the prosperity of the 1950s and 1960s turned into the stagnation and decay of the 1970s and 1980s. As the twenty-first century nears, the absence of a plausible corpus of economic theory becomes increasingly costly in terms of establishing the basis for effective policies

20. Alan Blinder, "Keynes, Lucas and Scientific Progress," *American Economic Review*, 77 (No. 2, May 1987): 131–2.

to mitigate the challenges ahead. The prospect for capitalist prosperity seems beset from many quarters – unprecedented international competitive pressures within the advanced industrial nations; horrific population pressures impinging on neighboring countries; exacerbated political instability with the decline of the Cold War; technological challenges to employment, to the environment, and to international peace.

Thus the stage is set – but set for what? In the absence of a new, constructive orientation for economic theory, the coming decades may be years of growing intellectual disarray with all the unwelcome political consequences that such a disarray would encourage. But there is also the possibility for a more constructive outcome. It is this ambitious goal to which we turn in our final chapter.

CHAPTER 7

THE CRISIS OF VISION

I

We must undertake one last task: to indicate the direction in which economic thought must move to regain its relevancy. The previous chapter was a first step toward this end, urging a reawakened awareness of the importance of distinguishing economic inquiry from natural science and, in particular, of the discipline's integral connection with a capitalist order. Now we must attempt the more difficult challenge of spelling out, as specifically as possible, both the nature of the vision and the properties of the analysis most likely to give rise to a new and fruitful classical situation.

Looking to the future always presents its formidable risks, but perhaps we can gain some initial guidance from the broad metahistorical considerations of Chapter 2. There we noted that the history of economic thought, despite the often striking differences from one classical situation to the next, was nonetheless clearly divided into two distinct periods to which we gave the names Political Economy and Economics. The first, we recall, gained its character from the expression of an underlying aristocratic view of society manifested in the class-centered orientation of such otherwise different expositions as those of Smith and Mill. In similar fashion, the second period found its historical distinctiveness in the class-blind democratic political values that permeated classical situations as far apart as those based on Marshall and Keynes.

Can our metahistory serve as a guide for the future of economic thinking? Putting the question in that manner suggests that we are about to urge a return to the visions of Political Economy or Economics, with their associated analytics, to serve as templates for some Third Period to come. This is not, however, the direction to which our inclinations lead us. The lesson that we take from our metahistory is, to be sure, that classical situations arise from, and must embody, extra-economic considerations of a sociopolitical nature. But the considerations that shape today's sociopolitical setting seem to us far removed from those of both prior periods. So far as the view of Political Economy is concerned, one of its major assumptions – that the class of landlords will play a major economic role – no longer constitutes a consideration of importance for modern capitalism. Of even greater importance, modern-day assumptions as to prospects for the laboring class are neither so limited as in the earlier "classical" scenarios, nor so hopeful as in the Millian and Marxian socialist scenarios. Finally, for the reasons we have just described in the preceding chapter, it will come as no surprise that we find the naturalistic and apolitical orientation of the second period of Economics ill-suited to serve as the basis for a classical situation useful for our times.

What, then, might constitute the underlying framework for a new period of creative consensus in economic thought? The answer seems to us to lie in an area of concern absent from both earlier periods, but of central and unmistakable importance in our own. It is a recognition of the necessity for a widening degree and deepening penetration of public guidance into the workings of capitalism itself. Today, and as far ahead as we can see, neither the class dynamics of the first period, nor the problems of a universe of competitive economic agents seem likely to constitute the background assumptions from which will emerge the visions and analyses needed to frame relevant economic thinking. That assumption, rather, will be a newly appraised balance between the public and the private sectors in which the role of the former is considerably elevated over its earlier status. To put the matter in a more political manner, the essential background will involve a general recognition of the need for expanded public intervention to protect a capitalist order from the difficulties and dangers with which it will have to contend. It is the legitimacy of the public sector within capitalism that lies at the core of the contemporary crisis of vision.

There is of course nothing new in the recognition of the underlying bifurcation of the realms whence this viewpoint springs. Indeed the acknowledged presence, side by side, of two "sectors" constitutes an essential property of a capitalist order, as we took some pains to explicate in our previous chapter. So, too, the need to formulate, or to defend the need for public intervention has never been lacking in earlier conceptualizations. Here we recall Smith's limited, but not unimportant recommendations with respect to the "duties" of government, or Ricardo's urgings concerning the abolition of protective tariffs. And certainly a major extension of public intervention was explicit in the Keynesian delegation to government the responsibility for reducing unemployment. Nonetheless, in all these earlier visions, governmental intervention was depicted as a necessary but always subservient interference with the otherwise reliable workings of the system; we remind the reader of Keynes's assurance that his own theory was "moderately conservative in its implications" and that there was "no reason to suppose that the existing system seriously misemploys the factors of production we use."[1]

That assurance cannot be given for the period into which we are now entering. The causes for this new state of affairs are many. On the domestic front, they include a technology of rampant automation that has created severe employment strains in all advanced countries: The idea of "full" employment is today an objective to which not even lip service is paid. The result is prospective increasing dependency on government-financed programs of unemployment relief or

1. J. M. Keynes, *General Theory of Employment, Interest and Money* (New York: Harcourt, Brace, Jovanovich, 1964), pp. 377, 379.

public works. From a slightly different angle, the economic importance of public spending is also moving to the fore in the form of entitlements at all levels of society, from welfare, through social security, to health insurance. Collectively, these entitlements are now the most rapidly mounting stream of government expenditures. The trends are similar abroad, giving rise to difficult impending fiscal problems in all advanced nations.

Meanwhile, on the international front, new developments have dramatically enhanced the operational importance of the public sector. According to the United Nations Center on Transnational Corporations, over the last twenty years the number of multinational enterprises has risen from 7,000 to 35,000.[2] This "globalization" of production carries unsettling implications for all advanced capitalisms, including the lowering of social, environmental, and labor standards through the forces of market competition, and the rise of newly industrialized countries as major rivals for market shares. In a related development, the volume of international financial flows into the United States alone has grown to previously unimaginable levels. On a worldwide scale, this internationalization of finance seriously limits the ability of advanced nations to carry out domestic fiscal and monetary policies that are not compatible with the "will" of a stateless world financial market. On a still larger front, world population growth threatens to bring another billion people into existence within a generation, raising the specter of large immigration pressures for the advanced world, with serious consequences whether the flows are accepted or denied. Ecological problems on a global scale are already on the agenda of world affairs, and seem certain to increase as a result of heat and other emissions. And everywhere the forces of ethnic and nationalist unrest are apparent, together with sporadic terrorism.

2. United Nations Center on Transnational Corporations, *World Investment Report* (New York: United Nations, 1994).

All these, and related, developments are well-known, thus a confirming element in our contention that collectively they constitute the dominant sociopolitical background of modern times. By the same token, such developments represent a striking change in the realities to which a potential classical situation will have to accommodate itself. Let us therefore investigate the implications of our reading of the present background setting, first for the kind of vision, then for the kind of analysis, that will most successfully incorporate its assumptions within economic thought.

II

We begin with the requirements for a new vision. As with earlier classical situations, today's vision must incorporate the sociopolitical essence of the historical setting in its choice of the fundamental agents who will set into motion the economic drama itself. Having ruled out the tripartite class structure of Political Economy and the individual-centered Economics of the second, what is left to fill such a role? Our answer is the two sectors – not classes – that are at the focus of our present perception of things. In particular, our vision seems likely to incorporate the private sector as a relatively passive, although vitally important player, and the public sector as a strategic, although probably much smaller sector. The drama itself will then reflect a setting in which government policy plays a dynamic, determinative role reserved mainly for the actions of the capitalist class or the decisions of individual entrepreneurs. To our mind, this larger sociopolitical setting plays a background role as pervasive and important as did that of earlier class stratified, or later democratic–individualist perceptions of their respective times.

It follows logically that the overall scenario to which such a vision leads has a generally "dirigiste" flavor compared with those of the past. This more dirigiste orientation may assume many forms, as witnessed by the existing differences among Swedish, European, or Japanese variants of such a policy; and there is always the possibility that some capitalisms may seek to move in an opposite direction, the United States perhaps being the most likely candidate. But in our view, the vision most likely to form the basis for a new classical situation in economic thought in the advanced nations will presuppose a much more far-reaching application of governmental power, and a much greater recourse to government-sponsored social coordination than was acceptable in the past.

There is, however, a vitally important prior requirement for such an "institutional" vision. It is the express *legitimation* that must be accorded to the public sector. Here, a specific example may shed light. It is common to hear that undue government borrowing may "crowd out" private borrowing. That which is taken for granted in any such statement is that the social gains from the crowded-out private investment would warrant giving it priority over the public expenditure displacing it. Thus the prevailing – although tacit – view, especially in the Anglo-Saxon world, is the implicit superiority of private expenditure compared to public, with the exception of a reverse ordering in times of war, itself an illuminating point.

By way of radical contrast, the vision that suits what we see as the background reality of capitalism today calls for a very different valuation. If, as we have argued, capitalism is today a social order at bay before forces that require containment or channeling by strong government policy, the easy assumptions of the respective rank orders of private and public activity must give way to a much more considered approach. This concept emphatically does not mean that priority should now automatically be accorded to the public sector, as in the case of actual war. It means only that the older vision of public activity is no longer affordable – the "only" representing a potentially wrenching change in the vision that establishes the roles of the two sectors. It follows as well, of course, that not all government expenditures can be treated as consumption, that capital budgeting is essential for the public sector, however difficult it might be, and that the same cost–benefit scrutiny – necessarily from a social, not a private viewpoint – must on occasion be accorded to private as to public economic activity.

We remind the reader that the broad scope of a classical situation does not imply that there will be a single "correct" conception of the role of the public sector. Much will depend on developments that cannot be foreseen: the character of specific new technologies, the speed of advent of ecological threats, the character of the domestic political climate, and of course political possibilities and impossibilities that develop on the international scene. Hence, there can be no possibility of prescribing, much less predicting, the particular operational configuration that will emerge from a new classical situation. As we write these words, we are, of course, keenly aware that the popular view in America today is clearly in favor of a delegitimation of the public sector, not its enhancement. All we can do is reiterate our belief that fruitful economic exploration in our times requires a recognition of the increasing defensive position in which capitalism finds itself. This perspective already has considerable support in Europe, Japan, and a number of the newly industrialized countries. To the extent that today's clouds blow over – a possibility that we would welcome with joy – that prescription loses its cogency, and we would anticipate a diminished urgency to find a new center for economic thought, a state of affairs that would, in this happy case, be of much lesser importance.

III

We are not yet finished with our prescription. Classical situations depend on analysis as well as vision, and any change in vision is likely to put the process of analysis in a different light. The enhanced legitimacy of the public sector that we see as central to a new vision will require not only a change in the nature of economic analysis but also a transformation of the status of analysis in economic inquiry generally.

Considered as a purely formal act, analysis involves only considerations that we have already mentioned: an examination of the consistency of arguments, of the reliability of statistical methods for the assessment or manipulation of data, and similar largely apolitical criteria. The relatively minor role that formal analytics plays in the overall *construction* – not, of course, the working out – of theory thereby reflects the unproblematical nature of the role that it will play, either in deducing the consequences of the posits from which it begins, or in examining the definition of the givens that establish the original situation from which analysis departs.

Our assessment of the enlarged role of public policy affects this unproblematic status in two ways. The first concerns the use to which analysis is put. In the traditional construction of economic theory, analysis begins where vision stops, accepting the entities it presents, and proceeding to deduce the effect of any additional variable or variables by applying the powerful assumption of lawlike behavior to determine the causal chains that follow. An increasing reliance on political means to cope with internal and external challenges is apt to complicate, and perhaps radically to alter, this traditional theoretical sequence. The second effect stems from a change in the focus and purpose of theory itself. Given the strategic importance of government policy whose intent is to counter the "natural" course of events, the conventional predictive orientation of economics must change to what Adolph Lowe has called an "instrumental" – that is, means–ends directed – purpose.[3] This results from the use of analysis to infer the policy best suited to attain a necessary end result. The behavioral laws on which economics has built its formidable analytical apparatus ap-

3. Adolph Lowe, *On Economic Knowledge* (Armonk, NY: M. E. Sharpe, 1976); originally published in 1965.

ply only partially, if at all, to the selection of the means best suited to realize policy objectives, including some that may lessen some individuals' income.

As a consequence, the analytical function loses some of its erstwhile "sciencelike" ability to rely on underlying behavioral regularities, and takes on aspects of political and social judgment absent in the traditional application of behavior guided by simple maximizing. It is, in fact, this reorientation of economic theory that prompted Lowe to suggest Political Economics as its appropriate name, one that certainly accords with those we have chosen for past periods!

IV

All this presents the field of economics with an unprecedented challenge. The challenge is the inescapable requirement that economics must come to regard itself as a discipline much more closely allied with the imprecise knowledge of political, psychological, and anthropological insights than with the precise scientific knowledge of the physical sciences. Indeed, the challenge may in fact require that economics come to recognize itself as a discipline that follows in the wake of sociology and politics rather than proudly leading the way for them.

Such a reversal of the rank order of economics and its half-sister "soft" sciences would perhaps be the most unwelcome and indigestible consequence of the reconceptualizations that we envisage as necessary for economic thought. In today's conventional formulation, politics takes second place to economics, because economics is presumed to speak with the impartial voice of rationality in a context of an institutional association with political freedom, whereas politics speaks with a voice that has no presumed internal rationality and from a past too often associated with various forms of oppression.

It would be foolish to deny the ever-present dangers of political excesses, or to underrate the element of self-expression in much economic activity. But it would be equally foolish, particularly in these days of chaotic existence in the former Soviet Union or former Yugoslavia or in certain African nations, to overlook the equally horrendous possibilities that can follow from too little political order, or to deny that economic life in much of the underdeveloped world and too much of the United States offers little that promises even the most modest self-realization. Similarly, from our point of view it is equally shortsighted to extol uncritically the apolitical character or the disinterested motives of economics, insofar as our discipline, as we have seen, is intrinsically embedded in capitalism and to some degree thereby becomes its self-justifying voice, even when it is quite oblivious of serving that purpose.

In much the same fashion, to assert that economics, by virtue of its subservience to a clear-cut motivational directive and an affinity for a political climate of self-interest, takes precedence over politics is only to assert that a certain kind of politics, congenial with economic concepts and values, becomes the dominant value system of a capitalist order. It follows that if economics becomes an instrument for the attainment of politically chosen goals, it has not been "displaced" by politics, but has rather openly recognized itself for what it has always been, the indispensable servant of the sociopolitical order to which it ministers. This is no more than to say that sociopolitical forces are the foundation of every society, a statement that would be received as common wisdom in any society but that of capitalism.

In a word, *there is no such thing as an apolitical order.* There are only more or less reasonable, responsible, effective, and "just" organizations of collective human existence. A society whose economic activity is guided by politically self-conscious visions, and that utilizes means–ends analyses, will not exacerbate the ever-present dangers of a politicization of its life. It will only incorporate politics into the agenda of a society that wishes itself to be governed by its own choices, not by blind obedience.

Such a radical reorientation of our discipline is obviously unlikely today. Yet it is not impossible tomorrow. There is a small, but very deep dissatisfaction with the condition of contemporary theory, of which this book is only a small part.[4] If our general diagnosis and prescription depart significantly from that of more conventional expressions, the differences lie in two central elements that provide a fitting conclusion to our undertaking. One of these is our insistence on abandoning the natural law conception of economics and replacing it with the explicit assertion of the inextricable connection between economics and its underlying social order. Our second differentiating element concerns the necessity of reorienting the form of economic theory from prediction to policy guidance, a reorientation that emerges from our diagnosis of capitalism as essentially on the defensive before forces of its making, but not under its immediate control. Our hope is that those who may disagree with our specific proposals will join us in our overall assessment of the pressing nature of the case.

4. An unscientific sample of the recent literature of discontent includes E. Ray Canterbery, *The Making of Economics* (Belmont, CA: Wadsworth, 1987), 3rd edition; David Colander, *Why Aren't Economists as Important as Garbagemen? Essays on the State of Economics* (Armonk, NY: M. E. Sharpe, 1991); Herman Daly and John Cobb, *For the Common Good: Redirecting the Economy Toward Community, the Environment, and a Sustainable Future* (Boston: Beacon Press, 1989); Paul Davidson and Greg Davidson, *Economics for a Civilized Society* (New York: W. W. Norton, 1988); John Eatwell, "Institutions, Efficiency, and the Theory of Economic Policy," *Social Research, 61* (No. 1, Spring 1994): 35–53; Amitai Etzioni and Paul Lawrence, *Socioeconomics: Toward a New Synthesis* (Armonk, NY: M. E. Sharpe, 1991); Marianne Ferber and Julie Nelson, *Beyond Economic Man: Feminist Theory and Economics* (Chicago: University of Chicago Press, 1993); Geoffrey M. Hodgson, *Economics and Institutions: A Manifesto for Modern Institutional Economics* (Philadelphia: University of Pennsylvania Press, 1988); and Robert Kuttner, *The End of Laissez-Faire: National Purpose and the Global Economy After the Cold War* (New York: A. Knopf, 1991).

NAME INDEX

Index

Printed in the United Kingdom
by Lightning Source UK Ltd.
1466